~~Heroin~~ Heroine

~~HEROIN~~ HEROINE

The Journey Through Addiction, Recovery, and Self-Discovery

Chelzzz

Published by Game Changer Publishing

Paperback ISBN: 978-1-966659-03-7

Hardcover ISBN: 978-1-966659-04-4

Digital ISBN: 978-1-966659-05-1

www.GameChangerPublishing.com

Dedication

To my mother, may your loving spirit live on
through the unforgettable memories.

To my father, for all the times you've been my knight in
shining armor and the times you've been
my douchebag in tin foil.

And for my wife, Allison. For loving me through
the good, bad, and the ugly and for holding on
through all the hard times until I believed
in myself as much as you believed in me.

Read This First

Thanks for buying and reading my book.
Please scan the QR code to connect!

Scan the QR Code Here:

~~Heroin~~ Heroine

The Journey Through Addiction, Recovery, and Self-Discovery

Chelzzz

Recovery is possible...

It's a lifelong journey with no days off.

–Chelzzz

Foreword

Recovery isn't just about overcoming – it's about becoming. It isn't just about what you leave behind—it's about what you discover along the way. And it isn't just about mending —it's about transformation. True recovery is a journey pieced together from fragments of struggle, courage and vulnerability. Chelzzz's journey stands as an inspiring example of how darkness and pain can pave the way for redemption and hope—that there's always a pathway to a brighter future, and that there is beauty in the brokenness, and strength in the struggle.

Like Chelzzz, I understand the courage it takes to confront your darkest moments and transform them into a source of strength. As the founder of 12 Step Journals and the author of *The 12 Step Journal* and *The 12 Step Workbook*, my passion lies in creating tools that empower individuals to reflect, heal, and rebuild their lives with purpose and fulfilment. While my work provides structured resources for those navigating the Twelve Steps, Chelzzz has done something much more courageous – she's chosen to share herself. Her *real* self.

Her story captures the raw humanity of recovery, embodying the honesty and resilience I strive to encourage in others through my work. Both Chelzzz and I have drawn from our experiences with addiction, dysfunction and transformation to offer support to those still struggling. While my contributions are reflective and structured, guiding individuals toward clarity and intentional growth, hers are raw, gritty, and unapologetically real. Where I provide tools for navigating recovery, Chelzzz offers an unfiltered glimpse into the chaos and pain of addiction, laying bare the humanity and vulnerability that often go unspoken. Where I offer frameworks, she offers emotional truths. Together, our approaches reflect two sides of the same journey—offering both practical guidance and a deeply human connection to those seeking hope.

~~Heroin~~ Heroine is more than a memoir—it's a raw and unflinching account of addiction, co-dependency, and the long road to recovery. Chelzzz takes you deep into the chaotic and often heartbreaking reality of her life, peeling back the layers of trauma, self-destruction, and survival. Through her story, she offers a rare and honest perspective on the battles faced by those struggling with addiction and the complex dynamics of relationships shaped by dysfunction.

What sets ~~Heroin~~ Heroine apart is Chelzzz's willingness to go beyond recounting events. She delves into the emotional truths of her journey, shedding light on the internal struggles that often remain hidden. Her story is as much about redemption as it is about self-discovery, showing how pain can be a catalyst for transformation. With a voice that is both unapologetically real and deeply vulnerable, Chelzzz invites you to see yourself in her experiences and find hope in her triumphs.

This book doesn't just tell a story; it provides a lifeline. It reminds us that healing is possible, even in the darkest of circumstances, and that the path to recovery, though difficult, is worth every step. Whether you are someone on your own journey, supporting a loved one, or seeking to understand the complexities of addiction and recovery, it will leave you inspired and deeply moved.

In a time when addiction continues to devastate individuals, families, and communities, ~~Heroin~~ Heroine arrives as both a timely and vital contribution to the conversation. Chelzzz's story confronts the stigma and misconceptions surrounding addiction, offering a deeply personal and relatable account that humanizes an issue often reduced to statistics.

This book is particularly significant for those who feel isolated in their struggles with addiction or co-dependency. In a society that often views vulnerability as weakness, Chelzzz's raw and unfiltered narrative challenges that notion, showing how sharing our truths can lead to liberation and connection. Her journey resonates not only with individuals in recovery but also with loved ones seeking to understand and support them. It doesn't offer easy answers but instead provides the tools of perspective, compassion, and hope—encouraging readers to face their own truths and inspire change within their lives and communities.

As someone who's walked the path of recovery, I believe *Heroin* *Heroine* is an invaluable read for anyone touched by addiction, whether personally or through the experiences of a loved one. It challenges, inspires, and ultimately leaves you with the hope that no matter how far you've fallen, there is a way forward. Chelzzz's courage in sharing her story will undoubtedly spark courage in others to confront their own truths and embrace the possibility of change.

I encourage you to approach this with an open heart and mind. It'ss not just a story—it's an invitation to walk alongside Chelzzz on her journey through pain, resilience, and transformation. Her raw honesty and unflinching courage will challenge you, move you, and ultimately inspire you to reflect on your own life and the possibility of liberation.

As you read, let yourself be immersed in her experiences, both the triumphs and the struggles. Whether you're seeking understanding, healing, or hope, you'll find something here that resonates. Chelzzz's story is a reminder that no matter where you are in life, there is always a way forward—always a reason to keep fighting.

This isn't a book you simply read, it's one you feel. It's a testament to the strength of the human spirit and the beauty of recovery. Take your time with it, let its lessons sink in, and allow it to inspire your own journey of growth and transformation.

Let this book inspire you to take the next step—whether it's reaching out for help, supporting a loved one, or simply believing that transformation is possible. The journey may not be easy, but as Chelzzz proves, it is always worth it.

-Founder of 12 Step Journals
Author of *The 12 Step Journal* and *The 12 Step Workbook*

Contents

I can't lie, had some drinks and
popped some bottles of wine.
Told you I was doin' fine; I guess I lied.
A couple sips, to smokin' zips and blowin' lines.
I'm bouta slip I'm loosing grip of my own mind.
Can't see me comin' back this time,
I've been diggin' my own grave
since the first day I've been alive.
I was taught to numb the pain I feel inside.
Never let 'em take your pride.
Life's a fuckin roller coaster ride.
I know we all got our ups and our downs,
we just tryna hide the shame by fakin smiles.
Gotta fill the emptiness somehow.
Know I haven't been around.
Know I'm pushing you away because
I fear I'll let you down.
You were innocent, on the bliss of ignorance,
didn't mean to show you all the trauma I've been livin' in.
Didn't mean to bring alla the drama and the negative,
sorry for being so argumentative.
You want the truth? You're so perfect.
I can't fathom ever losing you.
Tell you things my actions never prove.
In a panic, feeling manic with my choices
and change of moods,
feels like I can't trust a thing I do.

Introduction

March 17th, 1993, was a cold and snowy day in Detroit, Michigan. My soon-to-be mother was as pregnant as one could possibly be, feeling more uncomfortable and tired than usual. By the beginning of her eighth month, she could barely move, in part because she used her pregnancy as an excuse to eat whatever and whenever she wanted, even when she wasn't hungry. As her ninth month began, the doctors told her she needed to stop overeating if she wanted to deliver a normal, healthy-sized baby. My mother, being her typical rebellious and headstrong self, ignored the doctor's advice. She came to regret that decision at 4:46 p.m. that day when she gave birth to a 9-pound, 13-ounce baby.

I guess I was just destined to be larger than life.

Looking back on my early years, I can only laugh at how ignorant and naïve I was. My imagination kept me occupied as a child and allowed me to disappear into my own little world, completely ignoring the reality around me. That's just one example of my childhood codependency. Those daydreams numbed me from experiencing the harsh realities in front of me.

At the time, I had no idea that my imagination would one day become a tool I would need to save my life on multiple occasions. I didn't realize I was codependent until my late 20s. When I discovered that codependency stemmed from my upbringing and wasn't just who I was as a person, I felt a sense of relief. It meant there was room for growth and change, and once I accepted that codependency was a significant problem in my adult life, I could begin to address it.

Codependents are often highly sensitive to the problems of others and have a deep insight into how to help them. However, this insight is rarely applied to their own lives. As a result, those who struggle with codependency often remain in the dark when it comes to navigating their own problems.

I was no different. I took care of all my significant others, beginning my role as a caretaker in childhood with my mother. I was able to provide financially for my partners, but I lacked the ability to meet the emotional needs of the relationship. I often feared that any disagreement would cause my loved one to leave, so I kept quiet when things bothered me. This led to me blowing up over trivial issues, creating fights so I could control the outcome. Someone once called it "writing my own story."

As a child and teen, my reality was extreme and overwhelming. I witnessed poor relationship skills firsthand while growing up. When I questioned my mother, she often blamed my father for her nasty remarks and uncouth behavior. When I asked my father about it, he denied anything was wrong, often saying, "It wasn't that bad." From a young age, my mother had me yelling at my father for things she was angry about, which damaged my ability to have a relationship with him until they divorced, and he was no longer living with us.

This is a strange form of child abuse—denying the harshness of reality and silencing the inner voice that tells you when something is wrong. My moral compass, so to speak, was damaged by caretakers who refused to acknowledge the problems they brought to the table. This eventually leads to silencing your conscience, leaving you with no control over what's happening to you or around you. This pattern creates victims in adulthood, as you begin to tolerate things that people with healthy boundaries would never allow. It also made it difficult for me to recognize other people's boundaries, often leading me to cross lines in conversations or conflicts.

Additionally, this caused me to block out feelings of pain and fear in order to avoid being hurt. It led to dissociation and detachment as I got older. I became disconnected from my own reality because facing it was too painful. I developed little to no self-esteem, and I acted out because of this, often hurting myself and those who truly cared about me. Until I realized I was codependent, I couldn't begin to build any real self-esteem. But by accepting this realization, I've been able to unpack the emotional baggage others had placed on me for far too long.

With the therapeutic help of this book, countless hours of reading and studying other books on codependency, and years of therapy, I was finally able to start shedding the burdens that had weighed me down for all these years.

I wrote this book in the hope of gaining more clarity on my own emotional and mental issues. It began as journal entries, unpacking all the baggage I had carried for too long. This book started as a way to free myself from the grip of addiction and break the lifelong bond I had with codependency. While writing, I attended NA and AA meetings as a newly sober addict in recovery. Hearing others' stories and seeing the same people discuss the same problems without solutions made me realize that my story could serve as a tool to help others facing similar hardships.

This book addresses addiction by getting to the root of the problem. It highlights the fact that addiction itself isn't solely to blame for why we behave the way we do. Our brains, hardwired as codependents, are often trapped in cycles of shame that weigh us down. Codependency leaves us drowning in a sea of negative emotions, and causes us to respond to them in ways that people with well-established boundaries find baffling.

In this book, we'll start at the root of the issue, offering explanations for why addicts of any kind behave the way they do and how to break free from these negative cycles.

Don't worry, you're not crazy... you're just codependent.

So here's my story—all of it: the good, the bad, and the ugly. I'm sharing my experiences in the hope that others won't have to struggle in the dark for as long as I did. My hope is that by reading this, I can inspire others to venture out into the unknown, discover their true selves, and live a more fulfilled life, enjoying the journey that much more.

Chapter 1

Through the Crack in the Door

There's a moment in every child's life when the world suddenly feels too big, too unpredictable, and too over-whelming. In that moment, the safety of familiar spaces and trusted faces is called into question, leaving a young heart stranded in uncertainty. For me, those moments came sooner than I expected, and they became a daily occur-rence, leaving me grasping for something solid to hold on to, or simply someone to tell me that everything would be alright.

During those years, I found myself navigating a maze of emotions I was too young to fully comprehend. I didn't have the words to articulate what I needed, nor the aware-ness to understand why I felt so vulnerable. But deep inside, I knew something was missing—something essen-tial that could soothe the constant ache of anxiety and fear. What I needed was reassurance, a steady hand to guide me through the darkness, and the knowledge that my feelings mattered. What I received, much like many others, was the complete opposite.

I heard my mother's muffled sobs through the crack in her bedroom door. She never shut it all the way, a trait that annoyed me as I grew older and became less inclined to deal with her mood swings and dramatic behavior. At about 6 years old, I remember things getting bad. Or maybe they always were, and I just don't remember anything before then. My mom and dad had always been heavy drinkers. I guess when I was born, my mom thought the party would end, and they would finally settle down. But she soon realized that drinking wasn't just a hobby for my father—it was a lifestyle that wasn't going to change.

It's true what they say about gravity: being pulled down is a lot easier than pulling someone up. I guess the same logic applies to life's situations. It's much easier to bring someone down than to help them grow.

I peeked through the crack in the door. Even at such a young age, my heart broke for my mom. "Mamma, can I come in?" I asked nervously. "Are you okay, Mamma?" She turned her red-eyed, tear-stained face toward me. I froze when I noticed the half-full glass of Pinot Noir next to two empty bottles on her desk. This was a clear sign it wasn't the "right time" to have a conversation. Yet, even though I knew I was walking into an emotional whirlwind where all bets were off, the part of me that wanted to protect my mom always outweighed my fear.

Walking slowly, almost on tiptoes, I approached her.

"Oh, Chels, my baby girl," she slurred, starting to sob louder. "Chelsea, Mamma needs a hug. Come hold your Mamma."

Those words were music to my ears. I never knew how she would react when I came to check on her—she was always so unpredictable. Hearing her accept me and want my love was all I ever wanted. I needed to hear it just as much as she needed me to hold her.

I climbed into her lap, wrapping my little arms tightly around her. I buried my face into her neck, petting her head and whispering, "It's going to be okay." As I started to say it for the third time, I could barely utter the words before I felt myself go flying onto the floor. Looking up at her, hurt and confused, her angry stare met my pleading eyes. "Nothing is okay, Chelsea!" she exclaimed, waving her arms dramatically. "Chelsea, we're poor. I can't afford to pay the bills, and we're going to be homeless. Your piece-of-shit father lost his job because he's a hopeless drunk, and now I have to start working nights just to pay for your Christian school. You won't be able to go to school with your friends anymore, and it's all because of your dad. We can't even afford groceries this week."

As a child, this threw me into sheer panic. Immediately, I began thinking of how I could help my mom and what I could do to get us out of this situation. As a 6-year-old child, I felt powerless and frustrated by my inability to fix things. All I could do was try to console her and treat my father like he was the enemy. After all, if she was painting him as the bad guy, he must be the bad guy. At that moment, I swore I would always be a better man than she said my father was, and I knew it was my job to take care of my mother. After all, she always told me, "I love you forever, I like you for always, as long as I'm living, my baby you'll be."

Growing up, I didn't understand the dysfunction around me. My mother was a codependent, a love addict, and an alcoholic—a lethal combination, as I came to realize when I discovered I had inherited the same demons.

I started to glimpse how bad things were at home around 8 years old, when my mom took a job at a bagel shop down the street from our house. My dad's drinking had escalated to the point where he stayed out most nights without even a phone call. Since my mom worked nights, I often slept on a small cot on the floor of the bagel shop, lying among poppy and sesame seeds, kept awake by the pungent smell of sugar, cinnamon, garlic, and yeast.

Since my father wasn't around to be a dad, it's safe to say he wasn't around much as a husband either. My mom made sure the bills were paid, handled the cooking and cleaning, and did maintenance of the house. My father cut the grass and did the laundry—that's about it. Frankly, if it couldn't be done with a beer in hand, it wasn't going to get done.

My mom's stress was too much to bear alone, so I often became the trustworthy confidant she lacked in my father. I was the one she discussed the bills with or talked about what we'd have for dinner. I was her marriage counselor, her weekend companion, her sleeping partner, and her voice of reason. For most of my childhood, I was my mother's spouse, while my dad got a free pass to do as he pleased.

As a kid, I didn't see how sick they both were. To this day, I feel guilt for airing our dirty laundry because I was taught not to do that. However, that's the codependency speaking—the shame they created that is no longer mine to carry.

As anyone would, my mother grew resentful, and instead of leaving, she poisoned the air even more with her lethal tongue, spitting fire at her foes and taking down anyone who opposed her victimized point of view. If you weren't with my mother, you were against her. And choosing to be against Rosie was like playing a game of Battleship and telling your opponent your coordinates. She was always the winner, and she always got the last word, leaving you sinking and pleading for life, drowning in a sea of brutal verbal attacks.

One evening, my mother was particularly flustered. She had a lot of irons in the fire, as she normally did, multi-tasking between cleaning, cooking, drinking, and various other activities crammed into a few hours. My mother would often bite off more than she could chew, attempting to accomplish everything with the best intentions but only creating more chaos and clutter. Around 9:45 p.m. on a Thursday evening, my father came up from his dark basement lair to address the fact that dinner wasn't ready. You'd think he'd have noticed my mom was at her breaking point, but as she often said, "Rick was fucking oblivious."

As my mom frantically tried to prepare the plates, my father began grumbling again about how late we were sitting down to eat. At that moment, everything moved in slow motion. My mom would get this look in her eyes when she was truly angry—it looked like she could shoot frozen laser beams from her pupils and kill you on the spot. And right at that moment, my father was destined to be vaporized.

My mother was holding her famous baked sweet pota-toes, slathered with butter and a delectable combination of cinnamon and sugar. As she plated the food, I saw her holding the scalding hot potato in her bare left hand—butter seeping through her clenched fingers and dripping slowly onto the floor—completely unfazed. "I'm so goddamn tired of everyone in this house. I don't even get respect from the dogs. Rick! If you want to eat so fuckin' early, then pick up an apron and—" SPLAT! With her left hand, she hurled the potato against the wall, causing an explosion of stickiness that coated every crevice of the blue and white checkered wallpaper in our kitchen. Gooey debris covered the floor, and we stood there, stunned and candy-coated. As usual, after causing a scene, my mom retreated to her bedroom, sobbing that no one cared about or respected her. She probably had a valid point, but at that moment, respect was the last thing I felt for her.

My father and I heard the bedroom door slam. We sat in silence for a few seconds before bursting into laughter. "Chels, let's get a pizza," he said to me, and suddenly, I felt safe. My father and I didn't bond often, but when we did, it was usually over trauma. Ever since I can remember, I've been a bit over the top—an eccentric, funny little weirdo compensating for my looks with my humor.

I got my sense of humor from my father. To this day, every time we speak, he tells me a corny joke to wrap up every phone call or conversation. When I was little, my dad would make up the most elaborate and intricate stories to get me through long car rides. I was always the main character, picking whichever friends or cousins I wanted to fight crime by my side. We were the kid detectives always stopping our arch-nemesis, Samuel Roosevelt. My father had (and still has) a one-of-a-kind imagination that could plunge you directly into the plot with every word.

One summer day, my dad took me to Cedar Point, the

coolest amusement park with the wildest roller coasters you could imagine. I was about 8 years old, and for the past few summers, I had been trying out the scariest rides at local and county fairs. I'd get my ride bracelet as soon as they opened the gates, and I'd be there riding until late at night when my mom had to drag me home. I'd always beg, "Just ONE MORE RIDE!" My dad thought that since I was conquering all the big-kid rides at the fair, I could handle a little more action that summer. So, we packed up the cooler early one weekday morning and headed to Ohio to become the "Ride Warriors of Cedar Point," as they advertised on TV.

My dad told one of his famous stories on the way to really set the mood and get my adrenaline pumping. He really knew how to kick off an 8-year-old's day. He chatted excitedly for hours until we reached the gates. My eyes lit up with joy and excitement when we pulled into the parking lot, which seemed larger than the actual park. As soon as we parked, I flung off my seatbelt and yelled for my dad to hurry up. He laughed as he stretched his legs, trying to keep up with an uncontrollably rambunctious second-grader. I used to do this thing when I got really excited, holding both fists by my head and shaking uncontrollably. It's probably safe to say at this point that I was practically convulsing in the parking lot, unable to contain my excitement.

Cedar Point was unlike any fair I had ever been to. This was like a fair on an intense amount of steroids. The rides looked scary as hell, and all the kids seemed much bigger than me, but I strutted into the park with pure confidence and swagger. I was wearing a great little pastel outfit with comfy matching jelly shoes, my ride bracelet was secure, and I was still hyped from all the crime-fighting against Samuel Roosevelt that had occupied me on the way there. I felt unstoppable.

As we walked briefly through the park to the first roller coaster, I was ready for some action. The Raptor had multiple flips and dips, flipping you upside down in every direction. A double flip! I had never seen anything so incredible in my life. After waiting in a long line under the hot sun, we finally approached the gates and stepped onto the platform. I kicked off my jelly shoes so I could feel the wind beneath my toes—God, I really am my mother's daughter. As we strapped in and our feet began to dangle below, I admired the view of the tiny, microscopic-looking humans passing underneath. I waved at the crowd like I was accepting an award, and before I could even scream "HI," we took off. I closed my eyes, yelling and screaming, loving the feeling of my stomach being left behind on every drop.

We went on a few more rides before I saw it. There it was, in all its glory: the most famous roller coaster ever—the Millennium Force. This was the one from all the Cedar Point commercials, the one with the biggest drop. This was the test of a true Ride Warrior. I ran into the line, only to be immediately stopped by a man checking my height. I just barely made the requirement. I started running into the line again but was stopped a second time. Apparently, everyone and their mom wanted to ride this, and the wait was 3 hours long. After hours in the excruciating summer heat, we finally approached the front of the line. As I looked up at the ride, it didn't seem to stop—it just kept going up and up and up. I wasn't stupid; I knew if it went up that high, it was going to come down. As an 8-year-old, I wasn't ready to take on the monster that was the Millennium Force.

My frustrated father decided to ride the roller coaster anyway, since we had waited most of the day to get on it. As he hopped into one of the cars and reached for the seat-belt, it seemed to be stuck. He pulled and pulled but couldn't get the belt over his waist. One of the ride workers told him he was too large to ride, and you could tell my dad was about ready to snap.

Moral of the story: being an adrenaline junkie will only get you so far. To conquer Cedar Point—and most of life— you need to be both mentally and physically fit.

As a student, I was far less "mentally fit" than my peers. I was overly intelligent yet under-stimulated, which led to a dangerous combination of boredom and energy. In third grade, I attended a charter school with classrooms in trailers outside the main school facility. I always found this a bit off-putting and questioned my parents' choice. Even as an 8-year-old, I thought it was strange to attend a school that could easily be mistaken for a trailer park, but I was too young to question the integrity of the setup.

The teachers were exactly what you might expect from a school operating out of a mobile home. My homeroom teacher, Ms. Hoover, was a fresh-faced young woman who immediately caught my attention. I had a huge crush on her, and looking back, I behaved like any young boy yearning for the attention of a pretty girl, acting out and misbehaving just to get her to notice me.

In third grade, my mother started to notice that I wasn't outgrowing my chaotic behavior and random outbursts in class. I often failed to raise my hand before shouting out an answer, my desk was constantly disorganized, and I was far louder than the average student. Ms. Hoover began sending notes home frequently, which finally prompted my mother to get me tested for ADHD. I passed with flying colors. It was well into my third-grade year that I received my diagnosis, so I spent most of that school year struggling with self-control while unmedicated.

Ms. Hoover didn't believe in homework, mostly because she couldn't be bothered to grade it. Most of that year, I spent my time playing and chatting with peers, and school became more of a social hour. There were rare occasions, however, when Ms. Hoover actually felt like teaching us. On those occasions, I wasn't the most cooperative student, which resulted in a permanent seat with my desk facing the wall, my back to the class.

A few other students had similar ADHD-related issues and were also banished to different corners of the room, separated from the rest of the class with their desks facing the wall. "The Oddballs," she called us—a term that embarrassed me and left me feeling inadequate and ashamed. She would summon the class to line up for recess row by row: "Row one, row two, row three," and then, "All the Oddballs can line up." Day after day of being called an oddball really got to me, especially coming from Ms. Hoover, my crush.

I tried to get in her good graces once a week by bringing her a bagel from the bakery where my mom worked. She loved the asiago cheese bagels they had on Wednesdays, so every Wednesday, I would bring in her favorite. I'm thoroughly convinced I passed third grade for two reasons: one, Ms. Hoover didn't want me back in her class for another year; and two, the bagels.

Although we were all 8 and 9 years old and should probably have been reading on our own, Ms. Hoover would often read to us at the end of the day. She typically chose books that were far too advanced for our age group, filled with jokes and innuendos no third grader should have been reading or hearing, especially from their teacher. One afternoon, I remember her reading a story where a father and son jokingly flipped each other the bird. When the bell rang to go home, I confidently strolled up to Ms. Hoover's desk, flipped her off, and told her to have a good weekend. I couldn't understand why she looked so upset. We had all been laughing about it five minutes earlier when it came up in the story. I thought I was a genius for turning the joke back on her. At the time, I just thought it was cute and funny. But when I saw her face full of rage, I stopped immediately and was terrified. I knew I had really messed up, but I didn't understand the difference between reading about it and actually doing it.

I was genuinely confused as to how she didn't see that coming. Maybe I wasn't as mature as my peers, or maybe I just had a unique willingness to push boundaries. Truth be told, I was always the kid who would do anything for a laugh, and I could "read the room" even at a young age. If my jokes weren't landing, I'd switch to self-deprecating humor if all else failed. As a young, blossoming codependent, I either had a ridiculous amount of self-confidence or none at all. I operated on a plane of extremes, with no gray area. I was either all in or completely disconnected, and I always took things personally.

That was the first moment I can recall feeling extremely ashamed or embarrassed. When the bell rang, I couldn't run out fast enough. I saw my mom approaching the school, and I ran toward her, making a beeline for the car as fast as

I could. Just when I thought I was in the clear, a classmate named Bryon came up to me and my mom and jeered, "Haha, you got in trouble for flipping off the teacher." To be honest, the rest is a blur. There were tears and explanations. My mother was empathetic and could see I was truly shaken up. I think she was angrier at my teacher for reading that kind of book to us in the first place.

Update: Ms. Hoover has been divorced 27 times and now lives alone with her 40 cats. She spends her days on Facebook stalking her former students and enjoying asiago cheese bagels. She enjoys the peace of mind knowing she will never teach another child like Chelsea Henson ever again.

School was treated as a reprieve from life, as growing up in my household, my mother was either chaotic or controlling—there was no in-between. My mom was an amazing chef and baker. She could create masterpieces out of sweets, and her skills were highly sought after during most holidays. Because my mom never said no, she was often tasked with making a majority of the holiday meals and dishes. She would also take it upon herself to bring much more than what was required because "the foods paired well with the main dish." So, it never failed. Every birthday and holiday, my mother slaved away for hours in the kitchen to prepare a gourmet feast that only a few people would enjoy, as her overzealousness left us hours late to each event.

I often felt in the way while she was meal-planning and busy working in the kitchen. My mom seemed to resent the family and the holiday itself because she always went above and beyond. She would stay up late working on various desserts and then sleep in the next day, creating more time issues and chaos. During those times, you knew to just stay out of the way, or you risked Rosie's tantrums and theatrics ruining the entire holiday. When I was young, maybe about 8 or 9, I remember telling my mother I was hungry while she was busy cooking for the family. "Can't you see I'm busy cooking so you can eat later and have a good holiday dinner? God, Chelsea, grab something yourself and get out of the way."

I listened, feeling small and stupid for my request to eat while she was clearly prepping food for later. I walked to the cabinets to get a snack and settled on the fudge stripe cookies I saw hiding in the back of the cupboard. As I opened the package, my mother swatted the cookie from my hand. "God, you're just a junk food junkie! I can't believe you'd ruin your appetite with that when I'm cooking some of your favorites. Why do I even try for you when you're just going to insult me by going for the junk food like you always do? I'm making your favorite desserts, and you just want the junk." Her voice grew louder with every word until she was screaming, spitting in my red, embarrassed face, now stained with tears.

I left the kitchen with a belly full of shame to go with the hunger pains. The way my mother handled the needs of others was to ridicule you for having any, tell you to do it yourself, and then take over and criticize you for not doing it her way. I say "her way" because it took me a long time to realize that her way and the "right way" were two different things. There was nothing wrong with my way; it was just different from hers, and that was okay. But growing up, figuring out your own way of doing something was seen as a direct act of defiance. If you folded the towels wrong, it was a punishable offense.

As an immature and imperfect child, I learned that asking for help just opened the door to more verbal abuse and attacks, so I stopped asking. I aimed for the "Atta girl" in everything I did, and my self-worth came to be determined by my performance. I felt shame when I couldn't meet my mother's standards, and years of trying to measure up took their toll on me. By the time I entered high school, I no longer sought the approval of others and began to rebel. At least this way, I was responsible for my own failure.

I began to set the bar low and often did things that caused me more shame and pain as an "I'll show you." I was hurting myself because others had hurt me. I didn't realize at such a young age that I was already acting out my codependency. My upbringing made me feel unsafe when I tried to express my needs or wants, and it created an inability to see myself as someone who was allowed to make mistakes. I believed I was the mistake.

It was easy to say something was an accident when someone else was at fault, but when I was the one responsible, I was the problem. I couldn't view the issue as a temporary error that needed a resolution. Instead, I saw myself as the problem that needed fixing, so the issues always felt bigger because they were tied to who I was—or at least, that's what I thought.

Because of this shame, I have become anti-dependent in adulthood. This attitude and mindset are things I have to work on daily because the trauma is so deeply ingrained in my psyche. I've developed an inability to ask for help, even when I'm in tremendous need. The fear of being scolded for my requests is still very present, but today I am aware of its existence. Oddly enough, this awareness hasn't reduced my problems—it's only added to them because now I can see how immature I am due to what I was taught. But today, I see my immaturity as an area where I can grow and improve, instead of hiding it in the dark and allowing it to fester.

There's a heavy burden that many of us carry, often in silence: the belief that our mistakes are the truest measure of who we are. It's easy to get trapped in this thinking, letting the weight of past missteps and regrets shape our self-image. Each mistake, big or small, feels like a permanent stain, making it hard to see ourselves as anything but flawed and unworthy.

As we dwell on these errors, shame begins to creep in, wrapping itself around our thoughts and actions. It whispers that we deserve the pain we feel—that we are somehow less than others because of the choices we've made. This shame can be all-consuming, distorting our perceptions and leading us to become victims of our own pain. Instead of learning from our experiences and moving forward, we get stuck in a cycle of self-punishment, convinced that our mistakes define us and that we're powerless to change. The daily agony we face becomes the consequence of our "unbecoming" actions.

As children, many of us are taught that mistakes don't define who we are, and that they can be stepping stones to growth, unlocking doors to wonderful things. But growing up in my house, mistakes—especially minor ones—usually resulted in a chaotic emotional blow-up, leaving me feeling destined for failure. This left me constantly searching for ways to appease people and gain approval. When I realized I wasn't getting it from my parents, I began seeking it from my peers, my friends, and my partners—trying to make everyone happy except myself.

But what if our mistakes don't have to define us? What if, instead of being victims of our pain, we could learn to see ourselves with compassion and understanding? The path to freedom from shame begins with recognizing that we are more than our worst moments—that we have the power to rise above them and rewrite our stories.

Chapter 2
The Cost of Escape

As a child, I loved the water. I would swim at the peak of summer when the temperature hit 60 degrees. I'd spend hours playing in the lake at the cottage we rented for a week in the summer, and the rest of my time was spent at the public pool. I loved sports, though I was mediocre at most of them. As I got older, my mother pushed me to join the swim team at my new high school and encouraged me to swim over the summer at a local club team to get some practice. Most mornings, I spent practice fooling around with another girl who would be attending my high school. Sam and I quickly became friends, often goofing off at practice.

The only drills I paid attention to were the sprinting and backstroke drills. There was no doubt about one thing: I was fast, and my coaches began to notice, pushing me to swim at the summer meets. I respectfully declined and ignored the coach's guidance. I didn't realize how gifted I was at that moment, and I certainly didn't know that I had found more than just a hobby that summer—I had found my new passion.

In August of 2008, my high school swim team officially started its season with grueling running practices and some in-water drills early every morning. One morning, my coach wanted to gauge how fast each of us was with sprinting drills. We were to sprint a 50-meter length in 50 seconds, then 40, then 30. If we made it, we kept advancing to a faster lane. We did this until it was just me, one junior, and two senior girls in the sprint lane. I heard someone whisper, "Wow, Chelsea's fast." Coach Mazurek noticed my progress early on and worked hard to develop my skills. She placed me under the care of the seniors and our best butterflyer to help me improve my strokes. It wasn't long before I was keeping up with them and even beating them at times, and I began to truly love swimming.

During practices, I could sink into the water and think. It was the escape I longed for—a reprieve from the family dysfunction for a few hours every evening. Before long, my need to succeed took over, and I began pushing my body to its limits daily. I made it my goal to be the best, and before long, that goal became my reality. By my sophomore year, I was captain of my varsity team and swimming in the state finals.

My mom and dad loved coming to my meets, but their own battles with drugs and alcohol often led to embarrassment and humiliation. You'd think that their behavior would have been enough of a reason for me never to drink or do drugs, but instead, it became more attractive to me as I watched my peers start drinking and behaving the same way. It was a familiar and comfortable pain, one I had known all my life. It was unpredictably safe.

In my sophomore year, I was introduced to drugs and alcohol. I started partying with my peers and skipping practice. Swimming was great and all, but it didn't numb me the way the drugs did, so they quickly took precedence. I couldn't swim or do much of anything while intoxicated, so my swimming career came to an end as drinking and drugs began to take over my life. Bottom line: the drugs came first. You can't treat your body poorly and expect positive results, so I inevitably quit swimming my junior year to take up a full-time career in partying.

I witnessed this behavior firsthand and eventually began mimicking it. The desire to drink outweighed my love for sports. My mother's need to drink outweighed her ability to parent, and she often showed up to my swim meets drunk or in one of her usual moods. She created an astronomical amount of stress for me, as her support was more aggressive than nurturing.

As I got older, my mom's unapologetic craziness began to mortify me, and by the time I was 14, she was officially embarrassing. My mother was the epitome of someone who gave zero fucks. From her wardrobe to the things that came out of her mouth, she was always going to be her authentic self, even if that offended people—which it often did. My mother had a gift and a curse. Being authentic had its strengths, but more often than not, she was too adamant about sticking to her guns and would ruin relationships over differing opinions. My mom's point of view was often the *only* point of view permitted, and if you challenged that, you were in for a heated debate.

Growing up and testing everything and everyone, I often got the displeased side of my mom. We would argue daily as I no longer followed her ways blindly and began forming my own beliefs. Evenings would start out great but end in chaos as my mother's drinking triggered an argumentative tone, and I refused to back down.

I took up working at a local pizza place most nights to avoid the unnecessary drama. By this point, I was misbehaving on a weekly basis, and my mom was simply tired of trying to tell me how to live my life. And I was tired of her telling me to do better when she wasn't doing better herself. Luckily, by the time I got off work most nights, my mom was asleep. I took full advantage of the lack of supervision, and I began hanging out with friends after work to smoke weed and eat leftover pizza.

As my rebellion continued, I was turning my inner pain and turmoil outward with vengeance. This often resulted in me going to any lengths to make my peers laugh, avoiding the emotional pain that I was drowning in. My parents had recently divorced, and I was living with my mother, only seeing my father once every two weeks when he would come down to Paisanos, where I worked, to have dinner. When my father was living at home, it was easy to think he was the entire problem. Things had been stressful for a while, as my father had been unemployed and my mother was carrying the household. But in truth, things were never "good," or even "decent," between them. Alcohol was their first love, and the family fell further down the list as both of their drinking increased. Seeing this firsthand, I wasn't shocked or saddened by their decision to divorce. I actually thought we might all finally have better lives because the constant fighting would be behind them. When my dad finally moved out, I felt grateful and hopeful for some much-needed peace.

I quickly began to realize that my mother was the

common denominator in all of her relationship problems. As her anger and resentment turned toward me, I started to feel sorry for my dad, gaining firsthand insight into how damaged people behave. Her behavior left me hurt and begging for answers I couldn't find. In my pain, I often lashed out, making fun of my peers and turning others into the butt of the joke to feel like I had some power.

One Wednesday, when I was about 16 and a junior in high school, I was driving my own car—a vehicle I had bought with money I'd saved up from working, so it wasn't much to write home about, but it was mine. My best friend Christina and I were driving to her house after school when we saw a ceramic deer sitting on someone's porch. The deer belonged to the Whenburg family, an odd family with their own set of problems. Christina and I saw Brooke Whenburg walking home from school as we drove down the block. We stopped and started yelling at Brooke, poking fun in our usual asshole way. After she entered her home, I quickly parked the car, ran to her porch, and stole the ceramic deer. Brooke was watching out the window as I jokingly put the deer's butt to my crotch and pretended to hump the lawn ornament.

For days afterward, we taunted Brooke about the deer, telling her how sexy it was and how good it looked on Christina's front lawn. Brooke mostly ignored us, sometimes shouting back, "If it's so sexy, why don't you fuck it then!?" Goooooooood one, Brooke! This only made things funnier to us, and the taunting continued. By this point, Christina and I had been carrying on about this deer for well over two weeks. One day, after lunch, I taunted Brooke about her deer in my usual way, but apparently, I had taken things too far. Before I could finish my sentence, Brooke threw her books at me, pinned me against the locker, and punched me in the face. I looked right back at her, but instead of swinging back, I just stared into her eyes and laughed in her face. This enraged Brooke even more, and she ran off crying.

Stunned, and now the talk of the hallway, I went to algebra class and prepared for my afternoon nap. As I rested my head on the desk, Ms. Ladensack kicked it, as she normally did, and told me to wake up. "Yo, calm down, I just got punched in the face," I replied.

"Chelsea, I really hope you're kidding," she responded before returning to her lesson. A few moments later, the phone rang, and my principal was on the other line, requesting my presence in her office.

When I walked into Ms. Huber's office, I saw Brooke leaving the building with her parents. My principal quickly began yelling at me, lecturing me about making a girl who already had issues at home feel unsafe at school. I understood where she was coming from and felt horrible for pushing Brooke to her breaking point, but I still thought it was just a joke and that they were taking things too far. The school detective came to question Christina and me about the disappearance of the ceramic deer. He said he was going to charge us with larceny if the animal wasn't returned. The only problem was that it was the dead of winter, and the ceramic deer was frozen to Christina's lawn. We told the school cop there was no way we could retrieve the stolen property in such harsh conditions. That excuse didn't fly with Officer Lature. The next day, he came to Christina's house with a shovel to dig the frozen deer out of the ground. Christina and I laughed out the window as the officer pried the deer from the freezing earth. Just as we thought the deer might come out unscathed, the officer made one last attempt to free it. He succeeded—but the deer's head was wrecked in the process, and somehow the animal ended up with only one ear. Christina and I were suspended for three days, and Brooke was sent home for a "mental health day."

As time passed, my stealing escalated. Christina and I began going to the mall weekly, dressed in baggy sweatpants and sweatshirts, to steal clothes and accessories from some of the hottest retail stores at the time. I hid my new clothes so my mom wouldn't find out, often doing my own laundry when she left for work so she wouldn't question where I got the items.

One wintery Saturday, Christina's mom took us to an indoor water park close to our house. Christina and I drove separately from her mom, so that we could come and go as we pleased. After a few hours of playing around in the water, we decided we were going to hit the mall to grab some new gear. When we left the waterpark, it was blizzarding outside: the roads were slick, but we were determined. I drove like a maniac (as I typically did), running red lights and speeding on overpasses. As I began to turn onto the freeway, I skidded on the overpass bridge, hitting the side and immobilizing my car. I got out of the vehicle to assess the damage. My wheels were pressed against the wheel wells, and there was no hope of continuing our journey. Christina and I had been drinking most of the day and were pretty buzzed. We couldn't call anyone for help because they'd know I had been driving while intoxicated, so we parked the car in a warehouse parking lot and sat for hours until we were sober enough to call for assistance.

I called my dad (as I always did when big things went

wrong) because I knew he would handle it better. I made up a crazy lie that I had been cut off by a Ford Fusion and had no choice but to swerve. My father believed me and tried to reassure me that everything would be okay. He dropped Christina off at home and then headed back to my mom's house to take me home. My dad had told me he would pay to have my car fixed, so I felt a little better, but I was still terrified of my mother's reaction.

When I arrived home, my mother immediately tore into me about driving irresponsibly. I tried to fake cry and hugged her, telling her how scared I was. In that moment, she grabbed my face, smelled my breath, and instantly knew I had been drinking. I played it off, saying it was just Gatorade, and my father believed me. I then started crying hysterically, exclaiming, "I can't believe after all I've been through today, you'd call me a liar and a drunk!" My father caved into my hysterics and agreed to fix my car. I'm sure my mom knew the truth but simply wasn't in the mood to argue that evening. To this day, I have no idea how I truly got away with it.

It didn't take me long to realize that sex sells. At about 14, I started using my body to manipulate men into giving me what I wanted in that moment. My first experience with this was with one of my best friends, who went to a different high school. As a freshman, I had switched out of East Detroit public schools into a different school district. As I was making new friends, I was still maintaining the friendships that I'd had for years with neighborhood kids I had known most of my life.

Dan was a young boy who'd pursued me for years. I knew I wasn't interested in boys, but at this time, being gay was certainly not the "cool new trend," and it was often met with confusion and ridicule. I kept my sexuality to myself as an adolescent, knowing that it would be an issue for most people in my life. I kept quiet and tried experimenting with boys, which often left me feeling even more empty and disgusted than I felt beforehand.

One day during our mid-winter break, I got a text from Dan asking me to come over. This wasn't odd: Dan and I hung out all the time, and he had been one of my best friends for many years. So I pulled my bike out of the garage and started the four-block journey to his house. About halfway there, Dan texted me, *"Chels, can I pay you to give me some head? My girlfriend won't do it, and I know you'll help me out."* My stomach immediately sank. I had never had anyone ask me if they could pay me for sex before. I wasn't a prude. I experimented with boys, and that's exactly how I knew they weren't my cup of tea. I had even confided in Dan about feeling different. This text angered me: it showed me that, in Dan's eyes, I was no longer his friend, but an object for sale. I kept peddling with tears streaming down my face, freezing to my cheeks in the cold Michigan air.

When I got to Dan's house, I barged in and demanded this money he planned on paying me for my "services." I counted it and "got to work," I'm not sure why I agreed or how it all went down from there. Even though I knew I had options, I felt used and like I had no other choice. My code-pendency made me not want to disappoint my friend and made saying no very difficult. Trying to fight back tears and restraining myself from re-creating a whole Lorena Bobbitt scenario on this kid's disgusting dick. I can't remember if I even finished. I remember Dan going to the bathroom and me going into his cash box and taking everything that was left. He took something from me, so it was only fair. From that moment forward, my relationship with men became strictly transactional.

As I grew and started to develop physically, these scenarios continued. For years, I truly thought I wore the scarlet letter on my chest and that something was wrong with me, given the way these men behaved. I didn't carry myself like a slut. In fact, I dressed like a bum in high school, always wearing sweats and oversized clothes to hide my curvy, womanly figure.

The year I turned 16, I went completely wild. After my parents' divorce, with the house often empty for me to do as I please, I took full advantage of my independence. In May of 2009, a new hookah bar opened at the corner of my block. A few friends and I would often find ourselves hanging out there on Friday and Saturday nights. Sam, an older, heavy-set Arabic man, was the owner and operator of the establishment. Sam immediately began flirting with me and taking an interest in me. I, with my "fuck you pay me mentality," thought I could get some free stuff and some extra cash by reciprocating a little bit. For weeks, Sam didn't expect much. He would buy us liquor from the party store next door to his café and let my friends and I drink ourselves into oblivion every weekend.

I thought I had it made until the day Sam decided he wanted something in return. He asked me to come help him in the back. When I got there, he pinned me against the wall and stuck his 45-year-old tongue down my 16-year-old throat. I tried not to cry in situations like this. I needed to always remain in control. So I asked Sam to get me more liquor, promising him some love when he returned.

I explained to my friends what was going on, and we proceeded to rob his cash box when he left. We took about 300 dollars out of the box, and my friend encouraged me to kiss Sam, saying I was "taking one for the team." The make-out session quickly escalated as Sam realized I was robbing him. I guess he figured he'd get his money's worth, which makes sense from his perspective. We should have gotten out of there after we robbed him the first time, but we kept pushing our limits to see how much more we could get. I guess Sam was acting no differently. My personality changed entirely after this "transaction," and I was no longer the happy, bubbly, innocent teen I had been before. I felt tainted by life, and this marked the beginning of my journey into active addiction. From that moment on, I couldn't handle life sober, and I fell deeper into depression, struggling to find my way out from the bottom of the bottle.

At this point, I knew I deserved better than what was being shown to me and how I was allowing myself to be treated, but I didn't know how to stop being the victim. I also felt an overwhelming sense of identification with my past mistakes. To me, they weren't just moments of weakness or adversity to overcome—I *was* the problem. Because of this, I felt I didn't deserve to feel real love or experience any of God's grace. My past mistakes also provided a safety net of explanation. When I was acting out and being punished for my behavior, I was getting attention, and my mother's anger toward me made sense. But when I tried my best and still received her cold shoulder, it left me with a pit of emptiness.

I carried a lot of shame, and at that point in my life, I

didn't realize that I needed to dive headfirst into that hope-less abyss to confront my past and avoid repeating the same mistakes. The truth is, I was unknowingly setting myself up for years of despair and feelings of unworthiness that would follow me for over a decade. My choices trig-gered a domino effect, controlling my next move. I was operating on the autopilot of insanity, repeating the same choices and expecting different results.

To live a different life, you have to be willing to put in the work—willing to take ownership of your issues and rid yourself of the baggage others have made you carry on their behalf for years. It's going to be scary, but what's worse: living in the same predictable pain or feeling some temporary discomfort while evolving into a new person? That pain becomes familiar and comforting in the most dysfunctional way. It's a feeling of consistency we can rely on and recreate at any time. But that's taking the easy way out. We trick ourselves into thinking that the adversity we're creating is just part of daily life instead of taking the road less traveled. There's a beautiful poem by Robert Frost about taking the road less traveled. In it, he states:

"Two roads diverged in a wood, and I—
I took the one less traveled by,
And that has made all the difference."

Life is full of crossroads. For years, I tried to take the easy way out, the road everyone else was traveling. I hoped that following others' footprints would lead me in the right direction, but everyone's steps just made it harder to find my way back to my true self. I was lost in the shuffle, trying to find out who I was in a sea of pain and despair that I was re-creating. There were many times I started to walk the right path, only to be distracted or to give in to the will of my flesh rather than listening to the beat of my heart. You may try and fail, but the most important thing is that you get back up and keep trying. Once you know there's another, easier, softer, and more graceful way, it becomes difficult to go against yourself—because you know you deserve better.

Chapter 3
Drowning in Familiarity

There's a strange, almost paradoxical comfort in the familiar, even when it's wrapped in pain. Over time, we find ourselves drawn to the same kinds of people—the ones who, knowingly or not, inflict the same wounds we've carried for years. It's a cycle that is as predictable as it is damaging, yet there's something about the pain that feels almost safe. This pain, although extremely harmful, is something we know, something we've learned to live with, and in that twisted familiarity, we find a certain solace.

These unhealthy connections repeat patterns we've long since internalized, patterns that echo the earliest hurts we've experienced. We often become repeat offenders ourselves, allowing these series of unfortunate events to keep "happening to us," or sometimes a bit of both.

At this point in my life, I was too young to know who was safe and who wasn't until it was too late, and I didn't realize that I was attracting the worst types of people because I was being my worst self.

I wish I could say I learned from my past mistakes and never degraded myself or sold myself short again. However, as my addiction began to take root deeper and deeper, my negative behaviors followed and became more severe.

By my senior year, I was a full-blown alcoholic, drinking almost every night. I had quit all my sports teams and started working evenings at an Italian restaurant to support my habits. Early in my senior year, my best friend Christina's ex-boyfriend introduced us to Xanax. It was love at first bite, a love unlike any I had ever experienced before. I had never felt so peaceful in my life—pure bliss with not a single care in the world. No matter what was happening, I was okay. It felt like the heavens themselves opened up to give me a 6 to 8-hour reprieve from life. I was safe; I was secure. Even if something happened to me, I wouldn't remember. Nothing could hurt me anymore. I was numb.

It didn't take long for people to notice that I was basically a walking zombie. I no longer had opinions or cared about things that used to matter to me. My days were a blur, and then came the day I overdosed in high school.

The paramedics rushed me to the ER from my high school. My principal, who was not my biggest fan, sat beside me in the ambulance. I knew I had really messed up this time. With only two months left before graduation, I'd be lucky if I was allowed back at school. I was throwing away my entire future. Still, I didn't care. In fact, I was angry they had revived me. I told them I was just high and didn't see why they needed to ruin a good time, but my explanation was met with confusion and concern from faculty and hospital staff.

A few days later, my parents put me in a 30-day treatment facility. I was by far the youngest person in rehab. At the time, I couldn't imagine how someone could use drugs again after going through such a structured 30-day program. Who would possibly mess up after enduring the people, the food, and the rules? Well, that would be me... but we'll get to that soon.

The facility was a dual-diagnosis treatment center for people with both mental health and addiction issues. I was convinced I didn't belong there, and treated much of my stay as a vacation and social hour. I met a boy a bit older than me in the facility named Nick, and we immediately hit it off, bonding over bullshit about sports and girls. For the first time, I felt comfortable letting go and being myself. I confided in Nick about being gay, and he was incredibly understanding. We became inseparable and hung out every night.

One night, while playing cards, Nick and I found ourselves alone in the day room. He asked me if I was sure I was gay and if I wanted to "find out." He then undressed from the waist down and shoved his dick in my face. I immediately wanted to cry, but he pushed my head into his crotch and forced me to play along with his disgusting game. When he was done, he patted me on the head and walked away. Nick got discharged two days later. I was released later that week, and I used drugs with a girl from my treatment center the day I got out.

Feeling even more depressed than before and now unable to attend school, I spent my time in self-pity, drowning my sorrows with Netflix and the couch. My school allowed me to graduate, but I wasn't permitted to return after the overdose incident. My mom was constantly trying to get me to go to meetings, but I typically came up with excuses. One evening, she got tired of my laziness and forced me to attend my first NA meeting. To my surprise, there were many beautiful women my age who struggled with the same disease. Most of these girls had graduated to heroin—a drug I had not yet tried. However, as they shared their stories, I started to feel like I was missing out and hadn't tried everything there was to try.

My relapse after treatment was short and filled with guilt. After being exposed to a new way of life, even briefly, I now had a conscience when I misbehaved. I quickly got back on track and moved out of my mom's house into a halfway house in May 2011. I was living with seven other women and having the time of my life—breaking rules, sneaking out, and doing everything I shouldn't have been doing. Even sober, life was still a party.

One of the girls I was living with had a sugar daddy who paid her bills and gave her a few hundred dollars a week for her time. I was familiar with these transactional relationships and certainly didn't judge Margaret for her occupation.

One day, Margaret asked me for a ride to Greg's house, offering to pay me. I wasn't busy and loved random adventures, so I kindly obliged. As we drove past I-94 to the other side of 8 Mile, I noticed how drastically the homes changed. See, 8 Mile has a bad reputation, but a lot of people don't realize that right on the other side, there's a small, very rich pocket of mansions and wealth, as the city surrounding it decays in its shadows. Just beyond 8 Mile, Lake St. Clair and the Detroit River merge, creating a beautiful masterpiece of bustling city life and upscale scenery.

As we headed into the beautiful neighborhood, I was intoxicated by the sights and smells around me. It wasn't often that I found myself in Grosse Pointe, and the locals made it a point to try to keep people from the inner city out. The homes grew bigger and bigger as we proceeded, and I suddenly noticed how much my '97 teal Chevy Cavalier stood out like a sore thumb.

Margaret gestured for me to pull into a driveway that looked to be a mile long, leading to a home that seemed like seven of mine put together. As we parked, a jolly, bald, pasty white man with a goofy smile rushed out to greet us. Greg gave Margaret a hug and then turned to me. I saw his eyes light up with childlike excitement, and I couldn't help but like the guy—he seemed like a harmless dork.

Greg stammered, telling me I was the prettiest girl he had ever seen. As we walked into the enormous house, I noticed the various paintings and sculptures in the living room. His home looked like the Louvre. All the art in this house combined could easily pay for all four years of my college tuition. Greg offered me a soda and then pulled Margaret into the kitchen to speak with her privately. This didn't bother me—I figured they were discussing business. A few moments passed, and Greg slipped Margaret what appeared to be a few hundred dollars. Smart, I thought to myself: Get the money upfront so you can't get taken advantage of.

Margaret called me over and looked deeply into my eyes. "Chels," she said confidently and lovingly, like an older sister—which I guess she kind of was. Margaret was 27 and I was 18. We lived together. She was like a sister. I trusted her. She began to explain to me that she was on her period and that Greg wanted to know if I wanted to take her place, and that he'd discuss compensation with me in more detail upstairs in his bedroom. I realized what was going on: Margaret was literally pimping me out. This stung. My friend—another friend—looking at me like an object. I was angry, but I felt helpless. I reluctantly went upstairs with Greg.

He explained that he only wanted to cuddle naked and that he would pay me $1,000 for my time. He could tell I was nervous, but then again, I could tell that he was too. I began to undress and lay with him. He started talking to me and asking me if I knew that Margaret had set this up. I began to cry as I admitted that I didn't. He then took $2,000 from his nightstand and paid me. Tears swelled in his eyes, and he apologized.

Wow, what a kind man, I thought to myself. I got dressed and laid back down. I told Greg I would get to know him and we could spend time together, dining and doing various activities, but I would not sleep with him. Greg loved the idea of having some young arm candy, so I began to see him frequently.

One day, Margaret must have realized Greg was no longer interested in spending time with her, and she grew suspicious of our relationship. She confronted me angrily and rather aggressively one night in the basement as we smoked a cigarette. She reminded me viciously that she was the reason I had this connection, ending with one line that stings still to this day: "Chelsea, don't forget to pay your pimp!"

By the end of the summer of 2011, after seeing Greg weekly, babysitting full-time, working part-time at a diner in the evenings, and with the money I received for my graduation, I was able to get my own place. It was a small one-bedroom apartment for $500 a month, nestled between two major highways and close to school and work. I eagerly began decorating and designing my place on a very small budget. My mom was excited for me, helped me out, and even adopted a cat for me so I wouldn't be lonely. As I transitioned out of the halfway house, I stayed in touch with many of the friends I had made in the program and in the housing facility.

I got particularly close to a woman in her early 30s who lived in another one of the sister homes. We started hanging out weekly, attending meetings together, and became inseparable. Often, we'd plan to go to the gym but end up sitting in the parking lot of Planet Fitness for hours, exploring each other's minds. Melissa wasn't conventionally pretty, but her mind made her intoxicating. It didn't take long for me to fall head over heels for this woman and convince her to leave the halfway house to come live with me.

Melissa had a way of making me feel inadequate. She always mentioned wanting a man and not really knowing if she was gay. No matter how much I tried to please her, it was clear she was unhappy with me. Melissa often logged onto my school laptop to browse the web, as it was our only home computer at the time. One day, as I sat down to do my homework, I opened the computer and found horrible messages she had sent to men on Craigslist, seeking an open-arrangement type of encounter. I was enraged, sad, horrified, hurt, and confused. How could she do this to me? Melissa and I talked about it in detail and agreed to stay together, but she wanted to entertain the idea of bringing men into our intimate encounters. I was not at all comfortable with this, but losing her wasn't an option, so I reluctantly agreed. Melissa took me to swingers' parties but always got upset, because the men paid more attention to me than to her. When she realized her idea was backfiring, she was no longer interested in sharing, but she seemed to hold resentment against me for how everything went down. Melissa was, by all accounts, unsatisfied with everything life had to offer her, aimlessly searching for a way to feel better, to feel loved, and to be accepted.

One evening, Melissa started complaining about neck pain and asked if I knew anyone who had muscle relaxers. She swore she didn't want anything strong, just something to take the edge off. I called one of my contacts, got her some pills, and left for my shift at the diner. I've always taken care of the women I've been with, even if they were older than me or had more clean time. Melissa was no different.

During my shift, I let her use my car so she could go to the library and fill out some job applications. Hours passed, and I texted Melissa numerous times, receiving no reply. I grew worried. When 11 o'clock rolled around, after working a double shift, I called Melissa to pick me up from work. No answer. This was unlike her, and I began to worry. As the last one out, there were no coworkers around from whom I could hitch a ride, so I began the three-mile walk home.

About an hour later, when I arrived at our apartment, I realized that Melissa had my key. Jumping into a window on the third story wasn't an option, so I frantically continued calling her, hoping nothing bad had happened. I called my landlord to let me into the building. I could hear Melissa's dog barking as I rang the doorbell, but there was no answer.

Melissa struggled with mental health issues, so I was always afraid that her depression would get the best of her and that I'd walk into a crime scene one night. At this point, tears were streaming down my face. When I finally got inside, I saw Melissa passed out on the bed. I tried to talk to her, but her reply was inaudible. I realized she was okay —she had just taken all the pills I had gotten for her earlier. Furious, I grabbed a blanket and pillow and slept on the couch. The next morning, Melissa apologized profusely and admitted she had relapsed and didn't want to stop. She then asked if I would use with her because she didn't want to start over alone. Reluctantly, I agreed, and I was quickly pulled back down the desperate road of despair and deprivation. Just one choice in one moment changed me forever.

People will unknowingly drag you down to where they're at in life. Melissa didn't want me to use with her because she felt amazing about her decision: that it was a good choice and it made her feel better mentally, spiritually, or emotionally. Actually, it was quite the opposite. She brought me down to where she was because she didn't want to be there alone. That's what addiction does. It not only ruins the lives of those directly affected, but it also seeps in and contaminates all the people you love and care about. Truth be told, I was addicted to Melissa before I relapsed on drugs. I was facing a total death of self, as the little life that I had known was now revolving around the chaos of someone else. My identity was intertwined with someone who was backsliding abruptly and quickly. Because I had nothing to lose, plummeting back into the grasp of my addiction was a safe and consistent decision, and one I continued to make time and time again, as I was operating on pure insanity.

Chapter 4

Love as a Drug

Love, in its purest form, is one of the most powerful and fulfilling emotions we can experience. But for those of us who weren't properly nurtured, where love was conditional and something that could be withheld at any moment, love can become an addiction. This need to be loved, to be needed, can drive people to make decisions that are not just unwise, but which can be deeply harmful to their well-being.

In the quest to feel connected to others, I found myself acting out in desperation, following along with what others wanted and clinging to a relationship that was unhealthy. I was sacrificing myself entirely to maintain the smallest sense of closeness to the one that, at the time, I loved the most.

As I continued on a downward spiral, I had moments of clarity that kept me thinking I was on the right track. I was running off endorphins, and the love I had for Melissa blinded a lot of my ability to make cognitive decisions. Love went hand in hand with my addiction. It often dictated my addiction because, at first, before I was any kind of drug addict, I was addicted to love in any form I could receive. Melissa was the first feeling of the truest love that I had ever known, and I would have done anything for her.

Melissa was addicted to heroin, something I had yet to try. My first run with drugs included excessive drinking and popping Xanax bars, ultimately living in a black out until I was offered a reprieve. One evening after the relapse, I went to pick Melissa up from her new job serving at a high-class restaurant fairly far from where we lived. As I drove home from picking her up, I stopped at a gas station to fill up my tank. A man with an expensive Mustang convertible came up to me and asked for help. He told me he left his wallet at home and needed about five bucks worth of gas to get to his destination. I reluctantly obliged and helped this stranger out.

He gave me his number and a bottle of Vicodin for my assistance and told me to call him the next day so that he could pay me back. As I walked back to the car, confused and astounded by what just happened, I showed the bottle of pills to my significant other. Without any question, Melissa took the bottle from my hand and popped two of the long white tablets into her mouth. Without hesitation, I followed suit. As we drove home, I felt a warmth suffuse my body. I tingled. My mind was relaxed. Once again, I was numb.

A few months went by, and we were now using Vicodin on a daily basis. At first, they gave me unexplained energy. I was working double shifts at a bar and taking home almost $1,000 per night. All of it, however, was going to our habit, and I was now asking my dad to pay my rent for me every month. My family questioned the integrity of my relationship with Melissa. They saw me less and less, and typically, I only came around if I needed something. I began losing weight drastically and had no explanation for my declining physical and mental health.

At the peak of our addiction, we were running low on money to fund our habit. One evening, Melissa asked me if I still spoke to Greg. I told her no, but that I still had his number. She urged me to reach out. I warned her that if I called him, he wasn't going to just give me money anymore; this time, he would expect something in return. I was met with the same attitude I'd encountered before, the same one my friends had given me when I tried to tell them what Sam the hookah man had done to me: "Take one for the team."

This hurt more than ever because she was supposed to be the one who loved me enough not to suggest that. I saw Greg and got paid, but the money didn't last long, and my habit for a day was more than he was willing to cover. We needed another option. I began taking modeling jobs on Craigslist here and there. Some were decent, but others were incredibly degrading. Then I was contacted by a porn agency in Vegas that wanted to move me there to work in adult films. They asked me to come in for a paid audition and told me they had Vicodin if the audition went well.

I took Melissa with me because I didn't know these men and was afraid of being hurt. When we arrived at their house, she was more than willing to take over my audition. She wanted to sleep with the men and be seen by them, too. When she offered herself, the men kind of laughed and told her they weren't interested. This threw Melissa into a rage. After completing my "tasks," I came out crying, wanting to go home. The picture they had painted was far different from my actual experience.

I was taken into a back room with nothing but an air mattress on the floor and raped by five men as my girl-friend sat in the living room. Once it was over, I grabbed the pills and money and quickly left.

Melissa was angry, drunk, and belligerent on the way home, calling me a whore and telling me she didn't really love me or want to be with me. It broke my heart. All I wanted was love. All I needed was her. Why wasn't I enough? The argument escalated when we got home. Both of us were extremely messed up. All I remember is us taking pills and trying to kill ourselves, then waking up in a hospital. A few weeks later, I was put back into a treatment center for the second time, with another sincere attempt to get my life on track. Melissa and I broke up and stopped speaking.

A few years ago, Melissa contacted me and made amends for how she had handled the relationship. To this day, we still speak.

At 19, after my relapse with Melissa, I found myself back in treatment once more. It was a beautiful facility that bordered a lake and offered a tremendous treatment program. I was assigned a gay counselor who finally made me feel normal for my lifestyle, and I quickly made friends with other gay patients. For the first time, I felt accepted. Brighton Hospital earned its claim to fame after Eminem was a patient there in 2012. The facility was very high-end, offering delicious food, yoga, nightly tea, and meditation sessions. The beautifully landscaped grounds provided miles of wooded areas to explore. Meals were cooked to order; there was a soda machine and a nightly dessert bar. We were also allowed outside visitors, and our rooms had phones so we could keep in touch with friends and family. For an inpatient facility, it was very high-class.

After my suicide scare, I realized I didn't really want to die; I just needed a lot of mental health and substance abuse help. I took the program very seriously. I attended various groups and all the NA and AA meetings they had available on campus. I bought literature from their bookstore and spent my two weeks fully immersed in my own self-discovery.

Upon being released from treatment, I was doing well. Melissa and I were broken up, I was going to meetings, and I moved into another halfway house. This time, I was given more responsibility, becoming the house monitor and receiving weekly discounts on my rent for my help. My sponsor and her friend owned and operated the home. Stephanie was a very skinny and weathered ex-crackhead who was easily excitable. Jim was a short, fat, squirrely man with greasy hair who spoke with a raspy, low voice like he had just smoked a whole pack of Parliament Reds.

Being young, I enjoyed staying out past curfew and breaking the rules I was supposed to enforce with other members of the home, most of whom were much older than me. All of the girls were my friends, and combined with our age difference, this meant my position of authority was often undermined—rightly so, as I was joining in on all the chaos. We were allowed to have pets at this facility. I had two cats, and a roommate of mine had one young female cat that my male cat took an interest in. One day, while making coffee, I was laughing and giggling with my roommate, Sarah. We were carelessly spilling coffee grounds everywhere as we added them to the pot. I'm not sure what possessed me to do this, but without a second thought, I jokingly punched the coffee pot, sending it flying across the room. The grounds exploded like a brown, dusty rain all over the kitchen and our bodies. In a panic and out of pure laziness, I grabbed Jamie's cat and made little paw prints with her feet in the grounds. I then texted a picture to Jamie, telling her that her cat had knocked over the coffee pot and that she had a mess to clean when she got home. As funny as this was, I still feel a bit guilty about how that was handled. I hope Jamie gets a chance to read this because, to this day, I have still never told her it was me.

During this time, I took a job at Beaumont Hospital as a dietary aide and started making good money. However, I lacked the proper guidance to budget, so somehow, on rent day, I always came up short—a habit that my landlord was entirely fed up with. On the Friday of Labor Day weekend in September, I was planning my night ahead and fantasizing about the fun things to come. When I arrived home from work, I quickly realized my laptop was missing. I questioned all my roommates frantically as I searched for my missing computer. They all denied taking it, so I began texting Jim, asking if he had taken it. Jim replied, telling me I'd get my stuff back when I paid him.

Fury washed over me as I aggressively texted him back, calling him an asshole and demanding the return of my property. About an hour passed, and Jim still hadn't returned my computer. A friend of mine came over to help me calm down and suggested we go make a police report.

We hopped in my car and headed to the precinct. As we walked in, I began explaining the situation to the officers. They met me with kindness and were apologetic, willing to go the extra mile to help me retrieve my property. One of the officers suggested we take a ride to Jim's house to ask for the computer back. I agreed to get in the squad car, and my friend Heather followed in my vehicle as I rode in the front seat of the police car, casually chatting with the deputy.

As we drove to Jim's house, I started asking questions like "What does this do?" and "What's that for?" When I pointed to the computer screen on the dashboard, the officer asked for my license so he could show me how it worked. When he ran my license, I saw three things come up in red on the screen. The cop turned to me, looking puzzled. "Chelsea," he said, "you have three felony warrants out in St. Clair Shores for possession of analogs."

"What the fuck is an analog?" I replied as I saw him stop the car. At this point, we were at Jim's house, and my only thoughts were on my stolen computer.

"Chelsea," he stammered, "I have to place you under arrest. The Shores wants you."

My heart sank, a pit formed in my stomach, and I was paralyzed with fear.

Heather, who had a very public crush on me, rushed to my side, demanding answers. The cop placed my hands behind my back and read me my rights. This time, he put me in the back of the squad car and drove me to the border of St. Clair Shores and East Detroit. The cops spoke for a moment, and I was transferred to another car.

I was booked and processed in St. Clair Shores and placed in a holding cell with three other women, all of whom were very intoxicated. They gave me a McDonald's hamburger and milk for dinner. Stupidly, I didn't eat, not realizing it would be my last appetizing meal until the following Tuesday when I was released. See, it was a holiday weekend, so I had to spend a few days in lockup before I could go to court.

Hours passed before another guard came to the door to transport us to the main facility. I tried to hide my tears and act like none of this fazed me, though I was terrified. The officer opened the cell door and motioned for us to line up single file as he reattached the hand and foot cuffs. I received my one phone call before the transport and phoned my mom and dad to let them know what was going on. They were both frantic but trying to remain calm enough to reassure me that everything was going to be okay.

When we arrived at the main jail, I sat in a crowded holding cell for hours, just trying to sleep and check out. Eventually, a loud, masculine female voice called out, "HEN-SON," jerking me awake. I followed the officer to a room where I was told to remove my piercings and was questioned about my mental health. They asked me a series of questions, one of which was, "Do you feel suicidal?" I quickly answered yes, thinking they would take me to a psych ward or hospital—anything to get out of jail for the night. When the trustees handed out uniforms, everyone received a tan uniform except me. I was given yellow. I immediately convinced myself that I was being taken to the hospital. That must have been the explanation for the yellow jumpsuit.

More time passed, and I was greeted by a male deputy who asked if I was ready. Feeling confident that I was leaving, I jumped up and followed him up the stairs and down a dark, cold hallway. He opened a cell where I saw another girl my age sitting, making something out of toilet paper rolls.

"Where am I?" I asked nervously.

"Mental health section of the jail. Get in," the cop replied. Before I could say anything, the doors were closing and locking behind me. I realized I wasn't going anywhere —I was still in jail, now surrounded by legitimately mentally ill individuals.

Ida was a beautiful Egyptian girl. She must have seen how scared I was, and since she had clearly been there before, it made me feel safer. "Wow," Ida exclaimed, "you're so pretty, goddamn." I felt the same way about her, which eased my nerves a bit more. We talked most of the night. Around 4:30 a.m., a cop dropped two Styrofoam plates into our cell and yelled for us to get up and eat. I reluctantly picked through the slop he threw at us and settled for a wet chunk of cake that looked like the safest option.

Ida, with her mouth full of cold oatmeal, turned to me and asked if I planned to eat my breakfast. I pushed the tray toward her and buried my head under the blankets to cry a bit more. Why did I go to the cops in the first place? This is what I get for being a snitch. If I had just handled it on my own, I would have been fine. And where did these charges come from? Was it from the overdose in school? How could they not tell me this? So many questions went through my mind. All I wanted was my stuff back. God, cops aren't here to help—they're here to make their quotas. Fuck the police.

It was at that moment that I began to question not just the cops but everyone I had ever trusted.

When we're young, trust comes naturally. We believe in the goodness of others, relying on them to guide us and keep us safe. But as we grow older, something shifts. We begin to see the cracks in the foundations we once thought were solid. That's when we realize we have the power to think for ourselves, to make our own choices. It's a moment of awakening, but it's also fraught with danger. By the time we reach this realization, many of us are already carrying the weight of the damage inflicted by those we once trusted blindly. The pain, the confusion, the unresolved hurt —they all cloud our judgment.

By the time I realized I had a choice or felt confident enough to do my own thing, I was still left with a sea of pain and a whirlwind of emotions. The only thing I knew that could ease my anxious and fragile mind was drugs. Drugs started as a recreational thing because everyone else was doing them. They gradually turned into a temporary escape from my emotional pain, but at the time, I didn't understand how quickly things could escalate into a relentless cycle of dependence. What began as a way to numb the hurt ended up spiraling into something far more destructive, dragging me deeper and deeper into darkness.

At the time, I was too scared to address the roots of my problems—fearful that if I did, my whole life would come crashing down before my eyes. I didn't realize that was exactly what was going to happen as a result of not working on myself and only "half-assing" life the majority of the time.

Without addressing the root of that pain—whether through therapy, support from healthy peers, or other outlets—the reliance on drugs only intensified. The tragedy is that the longer this pattern continues, the harder it becomes to break free from it. What might have started as a way to cope with emotional pain can quickly become a source of even greater suffering—one that consumes your life and leaves nothing but damage and destruction in its path. The only way to truly overcome the cycle is to confront the pain head-on and seek out a path that leads you back to your truest self.

Of course, that's a lot easier said than done.

Chapter 5
Gravity's Grip

Gravity is tricky. What goes up must come down, and it's much easier to be pulled down than it is to pull someone up to where you're at in life. I learned this lesson the hard way in a lot of relationships. I tried to save the broken, to build without a foundation, to swim without a shore in sight.

Melissa was my first real relationship. I'm saddened to say that it was much more real to me than it was to her, and that's why I ended up getting my heart broken. She was the first instance of my disease of codependency running amok in my life—giving until there was nothing left to give, expecting love in return, and often retaliating with anger and aggression when I felt too vulnerable and used.

Until I was about 30 years old, I did not know what codependency was or who suffers from this uncontrollable illness that takes down its host and everyone around it. I had heard of these unfortunates before, but certainly, I wasn't one of them. It was easy for me to place the blame on others because they were older and should have known better—or at least that's what everyone around me was telling me. But even if they had the power to do differently and chose not to, I was still a victim of their circumstances. So, while the "why" might be important, it's never more important than the self-realization that urges change. I refused to let this journey victimize me again. It may have been their fault, but why was I choosing people who were faulting me? That was a journey I needed to take all on my own.

At 19, after my heartbreaking crash-and-burn breakup with Melissa, I was now confident that I was gay and felt a sense of security with this knowledge. I had come out to my mom and dad, and that was met with confusion and many questions, but I got the hardest part out of the way—telling my parents.

A few months after the devastating breakup, I began hanging out with another older woman named Heather. I was 19, and she was 30. Heather was borderline obsessed with me and went above and beyond to proclaim her love to me on a weekly basis. Although I wasn't attracted to her, she had a radiant personality and kindness, and we quickly became inseparable, hanging out every day.

Heather was supportive and helped me with money to pay for my probation fees and court costs that my recent case had racked up. She was living in a halfway house and working at Tubby's Subs, spending all her extra money on me while ignoring her bills and rent responsibilities. Heather was asked to leave the halfway house when her rent was 60 days past due. She was flustered, to say the least, when I picked her up from the house that evening, having been given 24 hours to remove herself and her belongings from the home.

Heather began venting in the car, frustrated and angry about her situation. I half-jokingly replied, "So what, you want to get high?"

Her eyes locked onto mine. "Yeah," she replied.

And before I knew it, we were heading down to inner-city Detroit to cop something I had yet to try—heroin.

When we arrived at the dope house, Heather had me wait in the car. I gave her my last $50, and she threw in her last $50 so we could get a bundle. When she came back to the car, she was ready to do the drugs we had just purchased. So right there in the driveway, we pulled out the baggies with the brownish-white powder. Heather laid out two big lines and handed me a dollar bill. I sniffed the dope off the center console and immediately felt an over-whelming sensation take over my entire body. I felt like I was in heaven—floating into the arms of an angel. I was safe, I was warm, I was more numb than ever before. For the first time in my life, I felt a sense of peace that I had never known. I knew at that moment that this drug was the only thing I wanted to live for. I wanted to feel like this every day. I had found a permanent escape.

We rented a cheap motel room in the middle of the hood to do our drugs for the evening. Heather explained to me that shooting up was really the best method to get the full effects, so we went to CVS, where I embarrassedly walked up to the pharmacy to ask for needles.

You don't know what dirty feels like until you have the pharmacist looking at you, judging you harshly as you pretend to buy needles for your diabetic friend. They know you're lying. They know what you're really using them for. And they always look at you with pity and disgust for your lifestyle choice.

As I purchased my needles and endured the walk of shame into the parking lot, all I could feel was excitement—a mixed feeling of my stomach churning like I had to throw up, combined with pure ecstasy.

After our night at the motel, I took Heather back to my mother's house, and we repeated what we had done the night before—shot dope, had sex, and fell asleep. We couldn't have been asleep for more than 10 minutes when my mother walked in and started screaming at me. She didn't know I had been using dope, but for some reason, she didn't want me in her home. This happened often after I moved out. Even when I was struggling, my mom wouldn't let me come back home. Once I moved out, I always felt like a stranger in her house and knew I wasn't welcome.

My mom was yelling and throwing my clothes into bags and boxes. Now Heather and I were both homeless, and we were both using. Talk about a recipe for disaster.

I phoned my father, who was used to getting me out of the problems I caused. He agreed to pay for a month at a motel so I could try to get back on my feet. Heather and I moved into the Eastin Motel later that day—a quick commute for her to work and for me to get high. Perfect fit.

I had recently lost my job due to my probation requirements. My color was called for drug testing, and I had to leave work early to drop. Because I worked for a corporate company, word got out that I was on felony probation, and I was let go.

I had nothing but time on my hands to sink deeper and deeper into my addiction and depravity. A month passed, and my father renewed my lease at the motel. My days were filled with shooting up, nodding out, smoking Newports, and waking up to burn holes in my clothes or small fires on the bed sheets from falling asleep with lit cigarettes. Heather was shooting me up because I was too scared to do it myself. She seemed to enjoy it—like she had some sort of control over me. I was getting tired of this and wanted my own freedom. I felt like she was holding me captive, so I began attempting to shoot myself up. Tying off with a phone charger, I carefully inserted the small needle into my arm, drew back a little to see the blood, and then GO. I had watched enough times to know what I was doing.

I had dropped a significant amount of weight in about a month and a half. Heather was working and occasionally stole from the register so we could get high. I had started a job as a nanny for a 2-year-old girl while I was using—something I still regret to this day. The family was welcoming and even wanted me to move in with them in their basement. The father worked nights and was often home sleeping while I watched the baby. They had some toys set up in the basement for Aurora to play with. Upon going down there, I saw they had a jar full of random bills—many twenties, a few hundreds, and a lot of ones. The jar had Aurora's name on it. While she was playing, I stole $300 from the savings jar, put the little girl in her crib, and left the home, never to return. I did a lot of shady shit when I was high, but stealing from a 2-year-old child was by far one of my worst moments.

Months passed, and I found myself unable to even look at the person staring back at me in the mirror. I hated myself and what my life had become. I was now working from the hotel as a cam girl—basically being a virtual stripper—making good money, degrading myself for an audience.

I had been running from probation for a while, and

warrants were out for my arrest. On Christmas Eve, Heather had taken a trip up north to see her family in Michigan. I stayed back at the hotel to do my dope in peace. The plan was to quit together after the holidays and for me to turn myself in.

When she returned, Heather was ready to quit. I knew I needed to as well; otherwise, I was facing prison time. However, I still couldn't escape heroin's nasty grasp. Despite my wavering attitude, I turned myself in and detoxed for five days in the county jail. I told my AA and NA friends about everything that happened between Heather and me, and they all said the same thing: if she really loved you, she wouldn't have introduced you to heroin.

It seemed so easy for her to stop, and that angered me. Why could she say she was done, but I couldn't let go? How could she leave me and make this choice without me when she was the one who introduced me to this way of life?

Upon getting released from jail, I was placed into treatment for two weeks before moving back into another halfway house. I knew I wanted a different way of life, but my addiction still lurked in the shadows, whispering and reminding me of my desires, suffocating me daily.

That's the thing about addiction—it can pop up and repeat the same patterns in different ways, with different substances, behaviors, and other negative outlets, still running and controlling our lives. We often ask ourselves when we finally feel so beaten that we need to surrender, "What's next?" I've tried to stop cold turkey, I've sat in countless meetings, hearing others share both negative and positive stories about recovery, and I've been given a label that defines my issue but doesn't offer me any reprieve from it. Some who can't face the pain and shame dive deeper into addiction, numbing any ounce of humanity left inside of them that attempts to crawl out. Addiction is only a symptom of the real issue. Until you can tap into yourself and realize that you're hardwired to repeat the same mistakes—and unless you're willing to pick yourself apart to put yourself back together—stopping the behavior is nearly impossible.

Sure, you hear of people living a life of abstinence but never delving into the issues that drove them to act out on their immediate wants and needs. They call these people "dry" addicts, living in a sort of limbo with no reprieve from cravings or guilt. Usually, the only thing keeping them clean is the immense amount of shame brought on by their addiction. But this isn't truly living. Adventure awaits when you explore uncharted territory. I never said you'll like everything you find; just don't get stuck there—stuck on the negative. Shame is a bitch, and it can creep in at any time. Your shame will tell you that you're not worth fighting for, that you're not good enough, and that you don't deserve the good that the world has to offer. That's bullshit.

I allowed those negative thoughts and feelings to control me for so long that I lost sight of what I was capable of becoming. Instead of allowing myself to grow and learn from my mistakes, I settled for what I thought I deserved. And that led me down the same path once again, with new people and new faces that were all the same.

Chapter 6
The Breaking Point

Heather clung to me desperately and did all she could to keep us together. The truth is, without heroin, I didn't need her, and I grew more resentful of her with every craving I had. Heather told me she had mixed up our needles by accident and had just tested positive for Hepatitis C. She reassured me that we could get through anything together and that this was going to be okay.

I hated her more than ever. Not only had she introduced me to my downfall, but now she was telling me we were stuck together because of her recklessness. As if it wasn't bad enough that the bliss of using heroin consumed my every thought and desire on a second-to-second basis, with no reprieve, now she was using an illness to try to regain my love and trust.

The truth was, I just wanted to get high, and Heather didn't, so we had nothing in common anymore.

After running from probation for a while, I was placed in a two-week treatment facility where Heather would visit and bring me cigarettes. I knew a lot of people in the center and quickly made new friends and acquaintances through swapping war stories and discussing the various drugs we were addicted to.

A butch lesbian named Jamie and I hit it off in detox. We were both heroin addicts with hefty habits, and we were both going through it. I had been using daily for months, and heroin has a funny way of shutting down the rest of your bodily functions. For most of the time I was getting high, I hadn't pooped. Imagine walking around for months without going to the bathroom. At the moment, I didn't care, but now that the drugs were gone, I felt like my ass was about to give birth. Jamie and I would joke and laugh to each other in between groups, asking if we had managed to poop that day. You definitely forget the small things when your life is consumed by getting high.

When I wasn't trying to poop, you could usually find me out back in the smoking section, shooting the shit with other patients. The walls were bleak, and the winter air stung the cheeks of the pickers and pushers as they desperately sucked on the butts of cigarettes they found in the garbage. "Pickers" and "pushers" were nicknames I used for the crackheads. Many patients were crackheads. Crackheads were a different breed. They were often much louder than those addicted to downers and had the most dynamic personalities. They'd flail their arms around while speaking and often disregarded people's personal space. They always seemed paranoid, even after they had stopped using. Tweakers. Permanent tweakers. And yet, all I could think was that this was another drug I had yet to try...

After getting released from treatment, I moved into my sponsor's halfway house. I knew I couldn't keep going as a heroin addict, but I had one foot in yesterday and one foot in tomorrow, and I was pissing all over today.

My fear of the future and shame from the past prevented me from living up to my full potential in the present. I was trapped in the prison of my own mind, drowning in a sea of self-esteem issues.

My dad had been paying my rent, and everyone around me urged me to get a job. I was tired of waitressing and wanted to find a career, so I applied as a vet tech at several animal hospitals in my local area.

I have always loved animals, especially dogs. When I first got my driver's license, I would drive to animal shelters to help walk and play with the homeless dogs that needed care and attention. I figured being a vet tech would be the perfect job for someone as compassionate as me.

It didn't take long to get hired at a very high-end animal hospital and shelter in a nice part of town. Serenity had waterfalls and ponds indoors and outdoors. When you walked in, it felt like an enchanting forest, with various animals roaming the hallways and greeting anyone who passed by. I was hired as a receptionist, so the job lacked its original appeal since I wasn't around the animals and had to deal with their owners instead.

During my lunch breaks, I would sneak away to care for the dogs we were rehabilitating—playing with them, walking them, and teaching them tricks. When we got new puppies from the kill shelters, I would assist in caring for them, as many came to us in very bad shape. Since I wasn't allowed to have a pet of my own, this was the next best option.

The no-pet rule was quickly broken when a woman I knew came into the facility one day with a kitten that desperately needed to be bottle-fed. She had found the kitten outside her home with no mother in sight and had brought it into the facility to be cared for.

I quickly grabbed the kitten and told her we could house it. The cat needed milk ASAP, and I wasn't going to turn this woman and the desperate baby kitten away.

A few hours later, I was taken into the office and fired because of my choice to save the kitten. I was also asked to take the cat home because we didn't have room to house it, and it needed round-the-clock care.

I obliged, not knowing what else to do. I brought the cat home and nestled it in a little cardboard box with blankets under a heat lamp. I fell asleep that night, waking up every two hours to check on the kitten. During the night, I woke up again, only to find that the baby felt cold. I picked up the small, lifeless body and realized it wasn't breathing. I lay there sobbing, feeling like a failure. Not only had I lost my job, but now it was all for nothing, and I didn't handle failure well. At that moment, I wanted to be the little kitten. I wished it had been me instead. Life felt hard and meaningless. Why would God let this happen when I was trying so hard? I wanted to trade places with the kitten more than anything. I wanted to end it all. If this was life, what was the point?

I was barely hanging on by a thread. It wouldn't take much to throw me off my square. After losing my job and failing the kitten, I felt lower than low.

I went back to waitressing at the diner I had been working at for years. My days were spent bullshitting with my roommates and doing favors for people here and there to make a few bucks.

One of my roommates was dating a girl who was in the treatment facility I had been in. Krystal asked if I could drive her up to Brighton to see Bre during visiting hours and offered me $50 for gas. I needed the money desperately and didn't mind Krystal, so I agreed.

When we got there, Krystal and I checked in and sat at a table, waiting for Bre. When she came out, we immediately hit it off. Our banter was unmatched, and we quickly made jokes, laughing so hard we had Krystal and most of the facility in tears.

When Krystal left to use the bathroom, Bre and I started talking about more personal things. We connected instantly. Our eyes locked, and I could tell at that moment we both liked each other. We had a moment. When Krystal returned, we chatted about Bre moving into another one of my sponsor's halfway houses so we could all hang out and attend meetings together. We exchanged numbers to "stay in touch and help each other stay sober."

Bre was released about a week later and moved into a halfway house where a few of my other friends lived. We had been talking daily in secret behind Krystal's back and had decided that we would be together once she broke up with Krystal.

The night before Bre was released, I demanded that Krystal take a drug test. I hadn't known she had been using Suboxone, but when she was urged to pee in the cup, she finally fessed up, resulting in her being asked to leave. Krystal was removed from the house in what seemed to be a series of perfectly unfortunate events. Unknown to me, just before Krystal was asked to test, Bre had called her to break up and told her that she was interested in me. Krystal screamed at me all night while packing her bags, throwing piles of clothes everywhere, screaming until she was foaming at the mouth, with a vein in her forehead bulging like it was about to burst. The 5'2" woman looked like she was going to explode.

I felt a mix of strong emotions—fear, pity, embarrassment, and victory. Looking past the fact that I had ruined Krystal's life, I felt like I had won. Bre had picked me, and I was about to find out just how much of a "prize" she really was—the hard way.

Bre and I began hanging out daily. She had the same crazy, fearless, thrill-seeking attitude that I did, and we were a perfect, diabolical, and destructive match.

Another roommate of mine was equally crazy. I'm not even sure how we came up with the ideas for the stuff we did. We were bored. It was winter in Detroit, with nothing to do. We were broke, young, and had nothing to lose.

One evening, I picked Bre up with Trina under the guise of "going to a meeting," which was code for us to drive around and fuck shit up. Trina had a new bright orange Mazda but never wanted to drive, so she always handed me the keys.

One night, hopped up on Red Bulls and Stacker energy pills, we headed down Gratiot Avenue into the inner city. We looked at the decay of the city in the urban sunset, noticing every crumbling building and all the destruction that surrounded our daily lives, often unnoticed. We turned down a side street where most of the block was burnt to the ground. We began exploring the decayed homes, looking for artifacts from the lives that came before us.

"Let's burn it all down," I said so nonchalantly that it almost gave me chills.

My crazy companions agreed, and we headed to the gas station, taking an empty 2-liter pop bottle with us. We filled it up with about three dollars worth of gas and headed back to the block.

When we pulled up, we realized we didn't have anything to start the fire with, so we all took off our undershirts and socks and soaked them in gasoline. We entered the home and began using the remaining gas to douse the walls and floors.

"Y'all ready!?" I exclaimed, and before they could answer, I took my Zippo out of my pocket, lit a gas-soaked piece of sock, and threw it into the middle of the living room.

"RUNNNNN!" Bre screamed as we watched the house quickly engulfed in flames. We stood there for a few minutes, just watching before we high-tailed it out of there. The three of us drove across the street to watch our destruction from afar. It took four fire trucks to put out the fire. We were mesmerized, and I quickly discovered the thrill of being a pyromaniac.

I was smart enough to know that this kind of manic and insane behavior often resulted in relapse, but I was always able to convince myself otherwise so I could continue with my mania, guilt-free. If I allowed myself to have a conscience, I would be crippled by the shame of my past and debilitated by the fear of my future. There could only be here and now. After all, they told us in the program, "Just for today."

It didn't take more than a few days of chaos with Bre and Trina before I started feeling the all-too-familiar urge to include drugs in the mix. I fought it for a few days, but one night, Bre and I found ourselves driving toward the city with only a few dollars and a burning desire to be numb.

Bre was a ride-or-die dope fiend who only cared about

herself. She could be amazingly selfless when sober, but that person seemed to disappear whenever drugs and alcohol came into play.

Bre grew up on a wealthy island west of Detroit called Grosse Ile. Her family had money, and she had never wanted for much. Most of her struggles were self-inflicted, and her mom was always there to rescue her—until the day she died.

The only problem was that this time, Bre's family was out of town, and the cash flow had halted once Bre was checked into treatment.

Luckily, when we got to the dope house, Bre's connect knew she was good for it, so we got to use on credit. Bre always told me that she was a fake heroin addict, that she really preferred crack and found it much more enjoyable. Bre stuffed a small white rock into a broken piece of pipe that looked blackened and severely burned. She hit the pipe, blew her smoke into my mouth, and had me do the same. Everything started spinning, and I instantly felt sick. I threw up a few times, then spent the rest of the evening begging for more. I was numb yet energized. Unlike heroin, it was a rush. What a ride. All I could think was: More. More.

We spent a few days sleeping in my car and living in the back of the dope house in a busted-down trailer. We spent our days having sex until we were both raw and exhausted; then, we'd get high and do it all over again. It had been a week, I hadn't showered or eaten much, and we were running out of credit with the dope man.

Bre came up with the idea of renting out my car to the dealers so we could continue to use for free. This lasted a few days, and my car was returned in shambles—making strange noises and barely able to start.

Bre said she had a friend who was using and would share some dope with us. By this point, we were starting to get sick if we couldn't get high. My skin was itching, I was nauseous, hot and cold at the same time, and extremely irritable.

We drove to a sketchy motel in Redford, Michigan, about 45 minutes from home, with no other options. My mom and dad had stopped taking my phone calls and had warned the entire family not to send me any money, knowing I was using again.

Bre got out and told me to stay in the car. We did the last bit of dope we had, and she went to meet her friend.

I'm not sure how long she was gone—I must have fallen asleep—but I was jolted awake by the sound of ambulance sirens. The EMTs rushed to the door where Bre had gone in. I watched them pull her small frame onto a stretcher after they revived her. From a distance, Bre waved to me as she was taken to the hospital.

I remember being mad that she hadn't shared with me —not concerned about whether she was okay, just angry. That's where this disease takes you.

The cops approached my car and told me they knew what I was doing there and that I was intoxicated. They warned me that if I drove off, they would arrest me. I called my sponsor, the only person who would still answer my calls. She came to my rescue and got me back to the halfway house safely. This time, I was so broken that I was willing to do whatever it took to change. At this point, I was ready to make a change but still very impressionable. I was ready to make the leap of faith and pull back the curtains to look out a new window, but the familiar faces and people who made me feel the comfortable pain kept drawing me back in.

Years later, Bre came back into my life. I'm not sure how Bre even popped back up. I guess viruses tend to do that—they pop up randomly and infect everyone around them. Once again, I fell for the facade that she was living a clean and sober lifestyle, and since I wasn't doing well financially, she seemed to offer a solution. She let me move into her place and taught me how to sell pills.

Although I wasn't using my drug of choice, Bre and I were both taking heavy amounts of Adderall and selling what we could on the side. This led Bre back into full-blown addiction, leaving crack pipes in our bathroom and disappearing for days to smoke meth with sketchy people.

I left Bre in the dead of night and never returned. It's a good thing I didn't go back. A few months later, I got a call saying that Bre had passed away. Some people don't make it out alive. Addiction isn't something to tiptoe around. If you don't get help, the price you pay is either your freedom or your life. That's the harsh reality of how many people's stories end.

Thankfully, by that time, I wasn't interested in using hard drugs anymore. I truly felt done, but I had no resources to start fresh and get myself going. I left Bre's house to live with my mom for a while. Her place never offered me peace, and I kept my stays there to a minimum because of the emotional damage I faced dealing with her. I eventually left my mom's and moved north, reconnecting with a guy who had paid my bills in the past. He offered me a place to stay, so I packed my bags and left.

With only negative connections and toxic relationships to rely on, I didn't have much of a chance to build myself back up. I moved back into the halfway house, aka "The Nut House," but without any substances to numb my reality and without a relationship, I felt empty.

My need for love and codependency kicked in once again like clockwork, and I found myself searching for another temporary high. This time, I thought I could find it through love rather than drugs. That led me down a path that showed me how ugly, toxic, and abusive relationships could be, looping me back into how I felt during my child-hood—scared, anti-dependent, and alone. I was bouncing back and forth like a pinball from the strong desire to change while still being jerked in all the wrong directions as I frantically searched for my own identity. I was ready for something new but lacked the tools and proper guidance to receive it, so I was left doing what I knew and repeating the same horrible cycles and getting the same horrible results.

Chapter 7
Tethered to Trouble

One evening, late at night, I received a message on Facebook from an intoxicatingly beautiful 21-year-old woman I had been trying to reach out to for quite some time. I was now living in her area, and she wanted to hang out. Kelly had long, dark black hair, tanned skin, and icy blue eyes. She was petite, with model-like good looks. To this day, she remains one of the prettiest women I have ever seen.

Kelly and I had gone back and forth for years on Facebook before she finally asked me to hang out. I had never set my sights on anyone as beautiful as her, so I was ecstatic when she agreed to make plans.

Kelly came into my life like a tornado. The first day we hung out, she was all over me. We would make out for hours, and she would just lay on top of me. She would fall asleep on me, and surprisingly, I could sleep, too. She *felt* like home. We would make love for hours, like nothing else existed in the world except the two of us. I felt something with her that I hadn't felt in any other relationship since Melissa—passion. I was definitely falling for her, but at this point, my guard was still up.

Kelly confided in me that she was using heroin, only a few days clean and very dope-sick. She asked if I wanted to go to the hood with her and do some dope together. For days, I held out, saying no.

One morning, I found Kelly doing my dishes when I woke up and walked down to the kitchen. I joked that I should "wife her up" because she was already so "domestic." She nearly broke the plate, turned to me with a huge smile, and said, "REALLY?!" At the time, I thought it was cute, but looking back, it should have been a red flag. She came over and just never left—the typical lesbian relationship move. And so, my journey with Kelly KaBOOM began.

Kelly continued to press me about going to the hood to cop. She said she needed to wean off dope and really wanted to quit, but that she was sick and it was unbearable. I knew that feeling, and despite only knowing her for a week, I cared about her, so I reluctantly agreed to take her down to the hood so she could get right.

When she emerged from the abandoned, decaying-looking house, she got back into the car, and we drove back to the suburbs. We pulled over in a Hooters parking lot, which had a sketchy, unlit back alley that wasn't visible from the main road.

Kelly began mixing her dope, drew the solution up into the syringe, tied her arm off with a phone charger, and shot up in her hand. A little blood came out, and she licked it off. "Do you want some, babe?" she asked. "I want you to feel good with me."

I had been sober for over a year from dope. I don't know if I just wanted to please her or if I really wanted to use at that moment, but without too much thought, I prepared my mix, took her needle, and shot myself up. Blood started pouring from the poke mark, trickling down my forearm. Kelly looked me in the eyes and licked the blood off my arm. It was so hot—so fucked up, but so hot. All the red flags—give them all to me. I wanted all her damage. I wanted to breathe her air. Suffocate me and bring me back to life. Love hurts, and she knew my pain. At that moment, I felt like whatever happened next was destiny as long as Kelly was by my side.

I stayed out using with Kelly for a few days before I finally had enough. I dropped her off at home and took the walk of shame back to my house to tell my roommates what I had been up to for the past week. They were incredibly supportive and told me to stay away from Kelly. I'll never forget what one of my roommates said that day: "You can be way up here," he said, holding his hand high, "and someone else can be down here," he said, holding his other hand much lower. "It's a lot harder to pull someone up than it is to get pulled down. You can't save everyone at your expense, Chelsea." Those words have stuck with me to this day because they hold so much truth. Basically, gravity is inevitable, and you can't give what you don't have. I found this out time and time again, but I was back to play the game once more. What I didn't realize was that the stakes were far higher this time.

I stayed away from Kelly for a few days before I answered her calls again. She told me she was willing to do anything to be with me and wanted to get clean for good. My roommates told me that if I stayed with Kelly, I would need to leave the house, so I began packing my bags to move into her mother's place.

Here I was, abandoning my safety to move in with a heroin addict and her mother. Typing this now, I realize how crazy I must have seemed to everyone in my life. How crazy I *was* being. I was allowing my codependent, love-addicted tendencies to run my life, and I didn't realize how much trouble that would cause me in the long term.

Kelly had plenty of run-ins with local law enforcement, had been to jail, and had done time on more than one occasion. I had only been to jail twice, both for very short stays after the incident I had in high school, and I had been off probation for about 18 months before meeting Kelly. However, that summer, I had racked up several speeding tickets, and my license was on the verge of being suspended.

Kelly and I were both very pretty and very lazy. Neither of us wanted a conventional job, but we desperately needed money. We started posting ads on Backpage and selling our services as a couple. I had this wild idea to ask for the money upfront and then rob everyone who tried to trick with us.

Kelly and I began meeting up with older men to do just that. I would make her sit in the car, tell the men to give me the money upfront, and say I was going to get her once we were paid in full. We would then drive away as quickly as possible before the men could catch on.

Sometimes, these transactions were so easy it felt like taking candy from a baby, but other times, I truly risked my life. One day, in particular, a man paid Kelly and me over $1,000 upfront, but when I told him I was going to get Kelly, he insisted on following me to the car. I panicked, unsure how I could get away. I shot Kelly a text and told her to pretend like she was crying so I could say I needed to talk to her for a minute. The guy still wouldn't budge. I then told him I had some outfits in the trunk that I wanted to wear for him, so he circled around to the back of the car and opened the trunk. I drove away as fast as I could, but the man had taken my bag full of pills from the trunk.

Kelly and I had many hustles. Robbing people was one, but selling drugs was another, and this man had just taken an entire month's worth of supplies—worth much more than what we had taken from him.

I didn't realize the pills were gone until I began driving away, with the trunk flapping in the wind. I thought we were in the clear when I noticed someone speeding down the freeway toward us. It was the old man trying to cause an accident by swerving his car next to ours to veer us off the road. I floored it and took the shoulder toward the city. This man wasn't going to follow me all the way to the hood. When I got to the Outer Drive exit, probably about 30 miles south of where we started, he was still on my tail. I exited and drove him around the hood until we finally lost him.

Adrenaline pumping through my body, I went to shut the trunk and discovered the pills were missing. This was a serious problem. We couldn't afford to lose a month's worth of pills due to carelessness.

I texted the old man and told him if he gave me my pills back, I would give him his money back. The issue was that the pills had my address on the bottle, and if this man were willing to engage in a high-speed chase over $1,000, he would definitely come by my house. I needed to prevent that from happening.

I racked my brain for a plan to keep both the money and

the pills. I thought about asking for the bag upfront and then giving him the money, but I knew he wouldn't fall for that a second time.

Honestly, I don't even remember how I convinced him to give the bag back before getting his money. It was a snowy evening, and we planned to meet in a Walmart parking lot. I got into the car with him, and he asked why I did what I did. I didn't feel like explaining, and I didn't have a plan, so I panicked, punched him in the face, and ran back to my car. He started chasing me on foot. I jumped into the car and sped toward him, increasing my speed, and clipped him with the vehicle. I didn't look back to see if he was okay—I just drove away like the vigilante I thought I was.

The summer I met Kelly, I made a lot of new friends and connections. By this point, I had lived all over Michigan, and I had people in all four corners of the state that I could reach out to for help.

A rich friend of my cousin, Antwan, had started to take an interest in me. He would give me money and Adderall whenever I asked, so I reached out to him for some help. Kelly and I stayed at Antwan's place for a few days, cracked out on the Adderall he was consistently feeding us.

One evening, as we drove to pick up dinner, I was pulled over by a Northville police officer, who informed me that my license was suspended due to numerous unpaid tickets. They impounded my car and took me to jail.

Antwan paid my bail and got me out right away, and he paid to get my car out of impound, but my license was still suspended, and I had to pay to get it reinstated—something I decided to put off for the time being.

One evening, Kelly and I were running low on funds, so I

asked my mother if we could stay with her for a few days. She said no but allowed us to come over for dinner. In a panic, I decided to have dinner with her, knowing I could help myself to some cash from one of her hiding spots while she wasn't looking. This time, my mom must have known better because there was no money in her red zipped bag by her bedside table. I did, however, find her checkbook and proceeded to steal two checks to make out to myself in the future.

My cell phone had broken earlier that week, and I desperately needed money to fix it, so I cashed the first check for $170, hoping my mom wouldn't notice. I paid for my phone, and we headed to Southwest Detroit to hit a lick on a white boy for some weed.

It was a snowy night, with a lot of black ice on the ground. I mentioned to Kelly multiple times that I didn't want to do this job, but we were broke, and "no" wasn't an option.

I drove my '95 Lincoln Navigator up to the guy's house. He came up to the window and handed me the weed. I told him to hop in the back on the other side because "the door didn't work on my side," a lie I always told to give myself more time to pull away safely. I locked the doors as he walked around, and we began to take off. He chased the car and managed to grab hold of it, hanging onto the passenger-side mirror. Instantly, I felt the car sliding on the black ice with this large man attached to the vehicle. I tried to gain control, but the car slammed into a pole, snapping the axle and tire rods. The wheel was now flipping inward, and I was barely able to drive. We made it away and parked a few blocks over. I called a tow truck and told Kelly to hide under the dashboard so that if the guy came looking for us, he would think we abandoned the vehicle.

About an hour passed, and there was still no sign of the tow truck. We thought we were in the clear, but I told Kelly to stay down just in case. She didn't listen and popped up to scope out the scene. At that moment, I heard a huge crash and felt a gust of cold wind come in from the back. BOOM! Glass shattered everywhere, with fragments filling the vehicle and leaving small cuts on our faces as the projectiles flew through the winter air. The boy's mother had just taken an ax to my back window, and the boy was violently punching at the driver's door. I somehow managed to drive off and called the tow truck driver, freaking out. At this point, he didn't even want to pick us up but eventually agreed.

The entire time the guy was strapping up the car, I kept looking over my shoulder, expecting the boy and his mother to pop out and kill us. Thankfully, they never returned. The driver towed my totally wrecked, unsalvageable truck back to the Eastside, where I spent my last $40 on a cheap motel for the night. At that point, all I needed was sleep. I knew when I woke up, I'd have to use that second check I stole from my mom to get us right for the week. That was the only option.

I opened my puffy eyes early the next morning. Sleep hadn't provided much of an escape from the harsh reality I faced. I was now not only homeless, but I had no vehicle and no money. No options... except the check.

Thank God for the continental breakfast that the Super 8 motel provided daily. Without that, I wouldn't have been able to afford to eat much. I sleepily crawled downstairs in just my boxers and sports bra to grab some food for Kelly and me. One thing about me is that I always kept my sense of humor, even in the worst times. I walked back to our room door with a bagel in hand and dropped to one knee. "Will you marry me, Kelly?" I asked, laughing. To my surprise, she looked me dead in the eye and started crying tears of joy, as if I hadn't just proposed with a motel bagel and stale cream cheese.

When the hype of the "engagement" settled, I sat in the room, ripping off little pieces of bagel and nervously eating them with cream cheese as I planned my next move. Between bites, I quickly dressed myself in a hot pink hoodie I had taken from Kelly, a pair of oversized gray sweatpants, worn-out Jordans, and blue boxers.

I had about a mile walk to the bank from the motel in the blistering January cold—not exactly what I'd call an "ideal" start to the day.

I headed out with my wallet, securing the check in one of the slots. I walked quickly as the frozen air clung to my lungs and turned my cheeks rosy. Panicked thoughts spiraled through my head as I replayed last night's epic fail. It was almost too painful to fathom. In the span of an hour, I lost everything I had—though it wasn't much to start with.

As I arrived at the bank, I put the check and my ID on the counter for the clerk to review. The clerk smiled, took both my ID and the check, and went into a room in the back, where he discussed something with another man. I was beginning to feel nervous and suspicious. The two men whispered amongst themselves for a few minutes before returning and telling me it would take a little longer to process.

I began to realize this wasn't typical protocol and demanded my driver's license back from the clerk. I started growing irate as my concern heightened. The clerk continued to smile and told me to "hang tight" and that it would only be a few more minutes. Just as he said, I turned to leave without my ID. I was much too suspicious to continue waiting. As I made my way toward the exit, I was stopped by four Roseville police officers. They questioned me about the check, and I denied everything. Then, they told me that my mother had filed a police report against me for the theft of the previous check and that I was being charged with three felony counts of uttering and publishing. My heart sank as my hands were cuffed behind my back, and I was taken into custody.

I spent the day in a holding cell, crying and sleeping. I was in holding at a local precinct for three days before they took me to the big jail to get processed and give me a court date. This was bad. Who could I call? Kelly couldn't do anything to get me out, and at this point, I was certain that my whole family hated me.

I took a chance and called my father, who, to my utter surprise, told me he had been in contact with Kelly and was working on getting me out. I couldn't have been more grateful. At the time, I felt selfish and entitled and really took my father for granted, but we'll dive deeper into that soon.

I refused to cry in jail out of fear of being targeted. I kept to myself and persevered. It took Kelly and my father ten days, but they finally got me out, and Kelly's mother allowed both of us to stay at her house when I was released.

Kelly was a hustler like me. She knew how to use her resources well. She arranged for us to have access to a vehicle as well as a place to stay. She definitely got things done.

When I was released, Kelly met me with a change of clothes and a kiss. We went into the bathroom of the jail, and she undressed me and began licking me all over. I had definitely never had sex in a jail before, but Kelly gave no fucks. She sloppily went down on me in the graffiti-filled jail stall until I finished. When we were done, she took me out to an old red Concord with a fat, jolly, bearded kid sitting in the front. "Get out, bitch," Kelly said to Robert, "she's driving," gesturing to me.

I hopped in the front, feeling like I had just carjacked this stranger. We headed to Kelly's house so I could get a much-needed shower, snack, and nap before we started plotting our next moves.

Due to my negligence and my alternative lifestyle, I spent a lot of 2015 in and out of jail. After Kelly got me out, I had racked up quite a few tickets for driving on a suspended license and failing to appear in court.

One Friday evening, my father graciously let Kelly and me stay with him in anticipation of a court date I had in his town the following Monday. He allowed me to use his truck to visit my cousins, so Kelly and I set out to hit the Northville Moose for a couple of drinks with my dad and cousin Chrissy.

We visited and proceeded to get pretty drunk. I laughed and had fun with my family and went out back to smoke a cigarette. My cousin's boyfriend, Josh, followed. I always made fun of this dude. He was at least 12 years older than me and reminded me of a hamster without ears. Short, scruffy, and unable to grow more than a few patches of fuzz on his cheeks, he had a weird way of doing things you just had to question. By all accounts, this guy was a total dork.

Josh came up to me, wanting to talk. As we spoke, Chrissy and Kelly joined us, chatting and laughing. Josh and Chrissy began to get into an argument, and without thinking, I pulled out a double-sided switchblade that I kept in my right pocket. I quickly popped both sides out so the blades were showing and held it up to Josh's neck. "We're leaving now, and you're staying here," I said to him with the knife to his throat. He looked like he was trying to act as tough as possible while fighting back tears. This guy was legitimately scared of me.

The power rushed through my body. I felt like a super-hero protecting the two women I loved from this irrational asshole when, in reality, I was the irrational asshole.

We drove around for a few hours, bar-hopping some more before we returned to Chrissy's condo. When we got back, Josh appeared at the front door, screaming and waving his arms frantically. "WHHHHHHAT the FUCKKKK, CHRISTINA?!" he was screaming, running toward the truck.

This upset me. Josh and Chrissy didn't live together, so why the hell was he in her house? In fact, it was her mom's condo. So, Josh had just broken into my aunt's house and was now throwing a fit.

Before I could even park the truck, Chrissy got out to try to do some damage control. I watched Josh and Chrissy fight as I parked the truck. Josh raised his arm above Chrissy like he was going to hit her and continued yelling at her, making motions like he was about to strike.

I wasn't going to allow my cousin to be treated this way in her own home. More screams were exchanged, and I watched Josh throw a bag of something down on the parking lot as they both fought to grab its contents. I couldn't see what they were fighting over, but I needed to act before someone got hurt.

I used to carry around a black spray-painted airsoft gun from Walmart that I could pull out if I ever got into some real trouble. This seemed like the perfect situation to prove my toxic masculinity and save the day with my souped-up squirt gun.

I hopped out of the driver's seat with my weapon in hand, walked straight up to Josh, and pulled out the fake pistol. In the dark, you really couldn't tell if it was a real gun or just a toy, and Josh was clearly shook. He decided he wasn't going to find out the hard way if this was a real weapon. After all, I had just pulled out a very real switch-blade on him hours before, so his guard was up for good reason.

Josh left Chrissy's condo, and we continued to drink until we passed out. Kelly and I stayed up that night, and someone came up with the great drunk idea that we should get married. It was probably my great drunk idea, but she excitedly went along with it. The next day, we packed up to head to Indiana to take full advantage of the gay marriage laws that were in place.

We woke up the next morning excited and nervous. Kelly and I packed matching Jordans, blue jeans, and white tees to wear while saying our "I do's." Certainly not traditional, but nothing about this situation was.

I didn't want to use my father's truck to drive to Indiana. I knew he wasn't going to approve of my marriage, so I didn't even ask for his help. I phoned Bert, who had been letting me use his car when I was out of jail. He was even using his car as collateral to get me out of jail, so I kind of felt like it was mine.

I found the title in the glove box early that Saturday and had a genius idea. I didn't need to borrow the car from Bert anymore—I could simply sign the title over to myself and keep his vehicle as my own.

Kelly and I headed to the Secretary of State's office early that Saturday morning to transfer the title. The only problem was that I had a suspended license, and I couldn't get a plate in my name. Kelly was surprisingly great at graphic design on the computer, so she whipped up a fake temp plate, and we stuck it on the back of Bert's car and headed to Indiana to tie the knot.

The drive was about four hours, and the car was in horrible condition. Every time we stopped, it stalled, and we needed a jump. A few days before, realizing this was an issue, I had stolen a battery jumper from Walmart. It did the trick to get us to Fort Wayne, but it was fully dead by the time we arrived.

I don't even think we cared about how we were going to get home. We sped the whole way there with a fake temp plate and a state trooper following behind us. We made it. That must mean we were destined to be, right?

As we filled out our paperwork at the clerk's office, we arrived just before they issued the last wedding permit. Kelly and I didn't want to get married at the courthouse, so we found a nice hotel nearby and met with an ordained minister in the lobby, where she performed our ceremony and took photos of us. My phone had been ringing off the hook during the ceremony. I saw several missed calls from my father, as well as from a state police officer questioning me about the gun I had pulled on Josh the night before.

My philosophy was: Ignore it, and it will go away. So that's exactly what I did. I phoned my angry father, who questioned me about the situation with Josh. "I don't know what you're talking about, but I just got married, and I'm trying to enjoy my wedding day," I told my father confidently.

"Oh, fuck, Chelsea, so you went along and did it, huh?" my father replied.

I met his disappointment with anger and frustration and quickly hung up the phone.

It was now late, and we needed to think about heading home. Kelly and I were hungry at this point, so we stopped at an Arby's drive-thru to grab some dinner. As we went through the drive-thru, the car died in the lane, and three Arby's employees had to come push us out. Talk about fore-shadowing the future of our relationship.

We waited for AAA and ate our dinner. They jumped us, and we drove home late without any stops. We spoke on the way home about trading in Bert's car the next day for some-thing more reliable. We decided we'd use it as a trade-in and get rid of it before he realized we'd stolen it. Now, as a married couple with a solid plan, I felt like we were unstoppable.

I lay in bed watching my new wife sleep peacefully. I felt a bit restless and remembered that the gun was still in Bert's stolen vehicle. This unsettled me, so I went outside barefoot in the snow to grab the fake weapon. Kelly had cut out a portion of one of her dresser drawers to hide her heroin long ago, so I placed the gun safely inside the false-bottomed drawer. Now I could go to sleep. I couldn't rest well if I felt there were loose ends that needed tying up. Nothing was more important than my safety. Now, everything felt right in the world. I closed my eyes to drift into my dreams and fell asleep beside Kelly, feeling safe and secure.

The feeling of safety and security was always something I longed for. Growing up in such dysfunction, when anything could flip at any given moment, carried into my adulthood. Mostly because I was becoming my mother, creating and thriving off the chaos around me. I just couldn't see it until much later.

As I awoke the next morning, Kelly was getting ready for court. We both had court that morning, but due to the many warrants out for my arrest, we decided it would be best if I stayed home and took care of the car situation. We agreed I would leave when Kelly left for court to head over to the dealership to pick out a new, used vehicle.

I quickly got dressed in a pair of Nike joggers, a gray long-sleeve shirt, a pair of Jordans, and blue boxers. Kelly and I headed out the door. She hopped in the car with her mother, and as I walked around Bert's stolen vehicle and unlocked the doors, I heard someone shouting at me from a short distance. "Stop, STATE POLICE! DON'T MOVE!" Before I could turn around, I was tackled to the ground by a fit older man with graying white hair in a state cop uniform. I was flipped onto my stomach and cuffed behind my back. Kelly and her mom had yet to pull off, and she witnessed the whole thing. She came running from her mother's car, screaming and crying, asking why they were taking me. "Gun charges," a cop said to Kelly. "We have a warrant to search the house."

Three officers stayed behind to search the home for the fake airsoft gun that I had hidden the night before. Another two officers escorted me 45 minutes west to the Northwood Police Department, where I was interrogated for hours regarding the fake firearm.

After hours of being pressured to succumb to their tactics, they gave up. All they found was the double-sided switchblade in the glove compartment of Bert's stolen car, and because the car was now in my name, they charged me with the evidence.

On top of this new case, my bond was revoked on the check fraud case. My father once again bonded me out from Northville, but I was taken back to Macomb County Jail in handcuffs to await another court date for the check case.

This time, I spent about 21 days in county lockup. I was in the general population, but I had my own cell. I spent a lot of time bullshitting and making new connections with people I thought could help me on the outside.

Kelly used the car title to bond me out with my father's financial assistance. I was free again at last. I swore up and down to my father that I would show up for court and do the right thing, but I didn't even know where to begin, so I went back to doing the only thing I knew how to do: scheming and making moves.

Old patterns are comfortable in an odd and dysfunctional way. As codependents, we cling to any familiarity and use it as a safety net. The problem is that people get caught inside this net and don't know where to go from there. This safety net is much like a spider web, full of past experiences, emotions, and memories that influence how we react and respond to similar feelings at different times. Many of us are foolish enough to think we are the master weavers of this web and can naturally find our way out. But we are not the spiders in this situation; we are merely the bugs trapped inside the fibers of our past, vulnerable to attack at any moment.

If you don't fight your way out, chances are you won't make it out alive.

This realization arrives at a different stage for each individual. As they say in NA, "Your bottom is as low as you're willing to dig it." For some more functional adults, it's easier to see a mistake but not take ownership of it. This means they take responsibility, but they aren't taking that mistake as their identity.

For those with trauma bonds and post-trauma from past experiences, this is a much more difficult task. We tend to take on our failures as our identity, unable to allow mistakes to occur without delving deeply into shame, pain, and anger.

This is where people without established boundaries typically hit a crossroads. You see, the pain they face daily is comfortably uncomfortable, and once you take away the drugs, all you have to focus on is what you did, what you lost, and what you gave away in your time of desperation and emotional depravity.

At this point, we can either surrender and search for a new way of life or revert back to what we know best. For me, my behaviors were setting me up to want to use. The scheming, the lying, the cheating— all of it. When I was sober, I felt so dirty and unsightly on the inside because I was still operating like a complete thug. If you only put down the drugs but aren't willing to change your behaviors, you're not only missing the whole point of recovery, but you're setting yourself up for a complete backslide.

They say in NA, every time you go back out, it's harder and takes longer to find your way back. When you keep piling shame on top of shame, along with guilt and pain, your cup is going to overflow with negativity and self-destruction. I didn't realize at the time that the side of me I chose to feed was the one that would find the light of day. When you keep feeding the darkness, you have no choice but to dwell in your own self-created sorrows. Let's be honest: addiction is a *self-created* sorrow. You have to be willing to find a part of yourself that is worth fighting for and grow from there. Addictions may be self-created, but the reasons why you use stem from various other culprits. We need to begin breaking these bonds, and often, we don't know where to start, so we fall back into the same old, terrifyingly comfortable lifestyle time and time again.

In these last few chapters, you've heard stories of me trying and failing several times. The same person respon-sible for all the negativity was also capable of creating positive things. It was at that moment that I began fighting back and forth with my addiction and the life I've always wanted. I got small reprieves from my past but only made half-hearted attempts to grow and mature. I was with someone who was actively using, and rather than sinking to her level, I began to compare myself to her. Looking into her problems and blaming her behavior for all the issues I was facing impeded my ability to grow because I felt infe-rior. This attitude stayed with me, and my arrogance kept me living the life of a dry addict. Only this time, I wasn't using any hard drugs to numb my reality... well, for a while at least.

Chapter 8
Love, Lies and Laundry Detergent

I remember one day sitting on the porch of Kelly's mother's house, smoking a cigarette and crying to myself. I hated how I was behaving and how I was treating people. Everything in life had become a transaction, and I only kept people around if they proved themselves to be beneficial to me. I couldn't bear being told what I was doing wrong, so if you weren't with me, you were against me. For a split second, I had a conscience, and all the robbing, cheating, and stealing I had been doing for the past several months was literally suffocating me. At that moment, I began having a seizure on the cold front porch, face down on the concrete.

I didn't realize until I was about 30 years old that I was acting out of control due to the spiritual abuse I experienced as a child.

Growing up, my mother was my higher power. Our relationship left me fearing authority figures and struggling to "people please" throughout most of my childhood, with these traits carrying into much of my adult life. She had an odd way of tearing me down when I tried to do things for myself while putting me up on a pedestal for how I treated her. In addition to that inconsistency, the rules in my household were often vague and contradictory, only adding to the chaos around me.

For example, my mom praised me when I made things for her or went out of my way to show I cared—likely because she didn't have a husband who ever did anything thoughtful. However, when it came to something I wanted to succeed in or took pride in for myself, like singing or sports, my mother would always find a reason to see the glass as half-empty, shutting me down and making me feel small.

She always had a suggestion for how I could have done things better or differently. This left me scrambling most of my life to give my all to others, hoping they would finally give me the "Atta girl" I'd always been seeking. As a result, I sought approval in everything I did, and if I couldn't get it, I would rather set the bar low. At least then, I could be the one in the driver's seat, controlling my own failure. The thought of trying my hardest and still failing crippled me, so I decided early on in my adult life that I just wouldn't try at all.

These inhuman rules and values became a part of my everyday life, leaving me constantly trying to achieve something that couldn't be achieved, which led to constant failure and shame. It left me not only feeling unloved and unworthy around the people in my life, but also feeling the same way with God. I believed God had rules and regulations I wasn't following, and therefore, He didn't love me, and I wasn't good enough to be loved.

I lied to myself and others to seem better than I was. I denied the truth to everyone, including myself, and lived in my delusions. I couldn't see that I was sabotaging my own life because, in my opinion, it was always everyone else's fault. I lacked any sense of responsibility or accountability for the life I was creating.

I stood at a crossroads: continue to blame others and remain a victim of my own circumstances, or take ownership of my life and grow up. This thought left me feeling hollow and inadequate as I sat weeping in the cold Michigan air, my tears freezing to my reddish face. And there I sat, hyperventilating on the porch of my mother-in-law's house, until I convulsed.

After spending my honeymoon alone in jail, the fear of going back was so overwhelming I couldn't even consider showing up for court.

Unfortunately, I had to return to Kelly's mother's house, and her patience with me was wearing thin. Her house had become a revolving door—if I wasn't there, I was locked up, and she was growing tired of our antics as the days went by.

At this point, I had been out of jail for a few weeks, still looking over my shoulder and still wanted by the cops.

Bert's car had completely broken down, and we had been driving it without brakes until one day, we had to crash it to bring it to a stop. Due to that mishap, Kelly and I were pretty much out of luck, quite literally sitting ducks.

One Sunday evening, Kelly and I were napping in her bedroom when I heard a bang on the door. Bill, Kelly's mom's boyfriend, answered and started talking to two men. I heard him say, "She's back here!" and immediately jerked awake.

"Kelly, wake the fuck up, hurry up!" I whispered.

We heard the voices coming closer, and just as the officers entered the bedroom, I was slipping on my shoes and jumping out the back window, running toward the woods behind the house.

I sprinted without turning back. Kelly texted my phone, letting me know the officers were bringing dogs to search for me in the woods.

I heard the dogs barking in the distance and knew I needed to conceal my scent if I wanted to get away. I dipped into a creek, removed my shirt, and threw it in the opposite direction of where I was heading. I then covered my face and body with mud to camouflage myself and make my scent more discreet. I found a large bush and hid inside for about two hours until they finally left.

Kelly texted me that the coast was clear, but the cops had made their rounds through the neighborhood and alerted the neighbors to call them if they saw me. I saw a young girl sunning herself in the backyard and I tried to run by unnoticed, but it's hard not to notice a skinny mud-covered figure running through your yard.

As I got back into the house, I jumped in the shower, and it wasn't five minutes before the cops were back at the door. This time, Bill and Linda had gone out to dinner, so Kelly and I turned off the shower and hid in silence until they finally left once again.

We knew we couldn't stay at Kelly's mom's anymore. We needed an escape, but the house was now being circled by the police every half hour.

I phoned my old roommates, who I had stayed with before meeting Kelly. I explained the situation, and, crazy enough, they told me I could come back and hide out there for a while.

At the time, I was selling drugs to make a living. I was seeing a doctor regularly who would over-prescribe Kelly and me pretty much whatever we wanted. My ex-girlfriend Bre's mother had a nasty Adderall habit and would buy my prescription for $500. She had phoned me that day asking for pills, so I told her if she could come to me (about a two-hour drive), I would sell her the pills at a discounted rate. I convinced her to also drive me over to my old roommates' place so that we could leave unnoticed.

This was the perfect plan. Bre's mom was Kelly's mom's age, and all they would think was that some old woman was coming over to visit.

When Bre's mom arrived, I told her to pull into the garage, where we discreetly packed up her car with our belongings. I sold her the pills and hopped into the back seat of her car, ducking down for the entire drive to my old house, fearful of who might be watching if I decided to peek out.

We arrived, and I felt a sense of safety I hadn't felt in months. For the first time in a long time, I was able to get some sleep.

It never dawned on me at the time that the only reason my old roommates accepted me back in the first place was that they were also using drugs and reverting to old behaviors.

All three of them had begun drinking excessively and partying on the boat almost daily.

At first, living there was fun again: long evening talks

with Kelly and my once-close friends, campfires, family meals, and the crashing sounds of the waves waking me from my sleep. I was back in heaven, but my bliss only lasted so long.

One of my roommates started acting odder than usual. He was beginning to lose his temper, and the slightest things would set him off. While cleaning the house earlier in the week, I found syringes in his bathroom and confronted him about it. He admitted, nonchalantly, to doing steroids and told me I had nothing to worry about.

One morning, my roided-out roommate woke everyone in the house up, demanding that they pack their bags and get out. He then left the home, leaving me in a panic. Where were we going to go? I was wanted for three felonies. I couldn't just leave and enter society. I was a sitting duck here, but at least I was hidden. Leaving this rural oasis meant leaving my only sense of safety behind. Not to mention, neither one of us had been working, and I hadn't been able to sell anything since we arrived, so we had about $100 to our names.

I liked to think I was quick on my feet in situations like this, but my quick thinking often left me with more problems to solve in the long run.

This situation was no different. In a split second, I had the bright idea to rob the house before we left. I knew where my roommate kept his jewelry and credit cards. I stole as much jewelry as I could find, a few bars of silver, snapped some pictures of his credit cards, and grabbed his printer. I called a few people for a ride to the pawn shop, and a woman who used to clean the house for my roommates and me reluctantly agreed to do so.

She always used to complain about my roommates, so I

figured I could trust her to help me out without getting told on. She took me to a nearby pawn shop, where I unloaded all the stolen goods. I profited about $160 from everything and booked a three-night stay at the Super 8 on one of the cards. Not my brightest idea, considering my roommates would now have my exact location, but that was a concern for another time. All I could think about was the here and now and the repercussions would have to be dealt with when the situation arose.

I received a text from my very angry roommate. All it said was, *"Not a smart move, sister."* Not a smart move indeed, but from my point of view, it was my only option at the time. He left no indication that he would be coming to the hotel, so I lay in bed, breathing nervously as I tried to get some sleep.

When I woke up early the next morning, I racked my brain for some "make money quick" schemes. We had no car, no drugs to sell, and very little time to act. The room would expire in two days, and we really needed to keep it moving if we wanted to maintain a low profile. After all, we were now staying smack dab in the middle of the dope and hooker hotels, and it was difficult to be low-key while on foot.

Kelly checked her Facebook messages and folded the laundry she was doing in the hotel facility while I sat plotting. "Someone wants to buy $200 of coke from us," she said confidently.

"Okay... but we don't have coke," I replied, confused and irritated.

"Yeah, but we could," she answered, more like a question.

"Kelly, how the fuck do you want me to make coke

appear from nothing? Do you want me to turn this laundry detergent into drugs? I'm not a—" and then it hit me. Laundry detergent. If I put the detergent in a cellophane and sealed it, I could run off with the money before the guy realized it wasn't really coke. And $200 could last us almost a week. We needed this lick.

I weighed out what appeared to be 2 grams of Tide, put it in a plastic wrapper from my cigarettes, and sealed it shut. I told Kelly to have the guy meet me in the back of the Super 8. Not the smartest idea to rob people from where we were staying, but I had a plan. Our room was on the 3rd floor at the front of the hotel. I would walk to the back, serve the guy his laundry soap, grab the cash, and run to the elevator before he realized what had happened. It was the only way, considering we had no vehicle.

So, I did just that. When I got outside, an older white guy in his mid-30s was with Kelly's acquaintance, a black guy who couldn't have been over 25. I thought it was an odd pair, but I didn't think much of it because the money was clouding my judgment. I gave them the fake drugs and retreated back into the hotel.

I wasn't in the business of making enemies, but desperate times called for desperate measures.

A couple of days passed, and we needed to make more money fast. At this point, Kelly and I could barely afford to eat.

For months, we had been dining and dashing at local restaurants just to eat dinner, but without a car, this was nearly impossible. By now, we were living off the free hotel breakfast and bags of chips and candy we stole from the gas station across the street from the Super 8.

Something had to give. I was exhausted, and my body

couldn't take much more of the ripping and running. Living this way without drugs was taking a toll on me mentally. My conscience could only act out of anger and entitlement for so long before I was flooded with guilt and remorse with no end in sight. At that moment, I wasn't sure what I feared more: continuing to live this way or what would happen next if I didn't.

Thankfully, I didn't have to worry about that for long.

Strangely enough, the man Kelly and I had sold the fake coke to reached out to us again. I was expecting to be screamed at or threatened for selling him soap, but instead, he asked if I could get him more drugs. He told me the coke tasted funny and asked if I had molly.

If this guy was dumb enough to come back and get robbed a second time, then I certainly wasn't going to feel guilty for selling him fake stuff. Honestly, I was relieved to hear he didn't die from snorting lines of Tide.

I racked my brain for what I could use to make fake molly. Pure molly is brown and sometimes crystalline, so I grabbed a few packets of sugar in the raw from the hotel's crappy coffee bar. I asked the front desk attendant for some glue. He looked at me for a moment but obliged.

I went back to my room and poured glue over a packet of sugar crystals, adding more sugar until the substance looked like brown rock candy. I crushed it a bit to break up the crystals until it looked enough like molly to pass it off.

About an hour later, the white guy came back alone and bought the fake substance. Just like before, I exited through the back and entered through the front, booking it to my room before anyone could figure out which direction I'd gone.

Another $200 made. This was getting too easy.

I spoke with Kelly as I got back to the hotel room, adrenaline pumping and sweat dripping from my pores in the late August heat. My best ideas always came to me when I was excited. My thoughts raced a mile a minute. I sat down on the bed, panting, and immediately grabbed my phone. I started messaging everyone who had ever hit me up for drugs, letting them know I had what they needed. I explained to Kelly that we should just keep going with the fake drug deals. Sure, we'd have a lot of enemies and couldn't stay at the Super 8 for too long, but this was a great system that I'd never really thought of before. If we had Tide, sugar, glue, or paper, we could make something happen.

The messages began pouring in, and we had over 15 licks set up for the remainder of the week. This was the break we needed to get back on our feet and out of the situation we were in. That night, I was finally able to sleep well. I didn't realize at the time that it would be the last good night's sleep I'd get in a while.

Kelly and I had plenty of money moves lined up for the week to get us back in a positive direction. The goal was never to live day-to-day or even week-to-week. But living the wrong way has a way of biting you in the ass, and all the money we had saved on several occasions had been used to bond me out of jail or pay court fines.

I woke up confidently, knowing we'd be secure for a while if I could make this work. A kid on Facebook had asked the evening before if he could buy a sheet of acid from me. This had to be the easiest scheme ever. Acid can take hours to kick in and is undetectable to the naked eye. All I would have to do was sell this kid a sheet of colorful paper, and he'd never know... until he did. By that time, he'd be blocked on Facebook and unable to find me. Plus, this was a $400 grab, and we could pick up and move our home base to another location for a couple of weeks with this kind of cash.

The kid texted me, saying he was waiting in a blue Neon outside the back of the hotel. I was getting good at this by now—making small talk, coming off nice and kind to throw them off, making them feel comfortable as hell before robbing them.

I got to the driver's side door and handed him the sheet of paper wrapped in foil. Just as I started chatting with him and going for the money, I heard multiple men shouting in my direction.

"STOP, FREEZE, HENSON! GET ON THE GROUND!"

I looked around and saw no police cars but spotted multiple men in police uniforms and street clothes pointing guns at me, demanding that I stop what I was doing and not resist. I scrambled over the Dodge Neon, Dukes of Hazzard style, and began running for my life. Within seconds, I felt my 110-pound body hit the hot concrete. My head must have bounced off the pavement because it was spinning. What the hell was going on? I had just been ambushed like a scene straight out of *COPS*.

As I tried to come to terms with what was happening, an officer looked at me and asked why I ran. He told me they could now charge me with an additional felony for resisting arrest.

"Additional felony?" I repeated, confused and a bit cocky. "For what, bruh? Selling your dumbass friend some laundry soap?" I smirked in his face and answered my own question. "What's my charge? Aiding and a-bedding? Get it, a-bedding?"

The cop laughed at my wit and replied, "Henson, you're being charged with three felony counts of delivering and manufacturing cocaine and MDMA. You're also under investigation for a home invasion, theft, and larceny in a building. You're looking at 11 new charges in total, and you won't be going anywhere for a while."

Robbing my roommates had come back to bite me in the ass. All this time, I thought I got away with it, but they were building up a bigger case against me.

I had been in and out of Macomb County Jail, catching break after break for the past 18 months. Not only was I looking at facing time for all these new charges, I was also looking at two years for absconding probation for the past several months.

The police told me if I allowed them to raid my room, they wouldn't charge me with anything I had in my possession. They said if I didn't allow the search, they'd get a warrant and charge me for anything they found. They lied to gain access to my room, where they found a pair of brass knuckles and other various weapons, which they also charged me with. They took the pile of money on the hotel room desk, snatching it up quickly. "All the cash we find is evidence, Henson."

Not only was I being arrested, but they were leaving Kelly with nothing—no money for my commissary, no money for phone calls, no money to live off of. Even money her mother had given us was taken as evidence of my crimes. At least I was going somewhere where I'd have a bed and three meals a day. Compared to how I was living, that didn't sound half bad. But my worry and love for Kelly and her well-being mattered more to me than my own security, and it would be days before I could speak to her again. Here we go again.

My obsessive love for Kelly was always what kept me going. I wanted—no, I NEEDED—that "Atta girl" validation, and when we were making money moves, she seemed so in love with me. That was the only thing I could cling to, convincing myself that how I was living was acceptable. It wasn't much different from the life I lived with my mother. In fact, most of the women I picked were very similar to her. Again, as codependents, we recreate the same patterns. So here I was, doing the same things with a different person that I had done my entire life. At the time, I just thought, "This is how life is supposed to be because this is how it's always been."

I didn't know there was another way out. I had been to NA, but I wasn't using drugs, and my life was still a mess, so what good would NA's clichés do for me in the real world? As I sat alone in a crowded holding cell full of people, for the first time in a long time, I began to pray. I immediately felt something come over me. God was blessing me before I could even understand how. I shortly found out that those "clichés" are the building blocks to creating a better future.

Chapter 9
Behind Bars, Beyond Myself

By the time I got back to jail, I had made a lot of enemies. I had robbed a lot of the girls in there, as well as their boyfriends, so I wasn't very popular coming back into county.

I had been locked up in D block for about a week, waiting for my court date and to be classified back into general population. D block was a hallway with 12 cells, each housing about 15–25 women. There was one shower and one toilet, and everyone could see you use it. I was in D8 this time, having bounced around and, at this point, been to each D block pod at least once.

I got friendly with a cute girl named Celeste while I was in D8. She and another friend from a previous jail stay would flirt with me and cuddle on the bunks. They gave me some of their commissary and helped me out from time to time until I got back into Gen Pop. Gen Pop was a much better way to "jail." You got your own cell with a desk, it wasn't overcrowded, you received your commissary quicker, and you were able to go outside. These two were staying in D block due to bad behavior. You couldn't get populated if you had gotten into a fight or had previous problems while in jail. Both girls were scrappy and had been sentenced to the rest of their time in D8. If they messed up again, they'd go to Max Security—24-hour lockdown.

There were a lot of ways to get into trouble as an inmate. You couldn't lay together or have sex, you couldn't be on another inmate's bed, you couldn't make wine—these were just a few things that could get you sent to Max.

I was tight with my D-block girls. A lot of them knew me and Kelly from the outside, and we were cool. It didn't take long for me to get into my routine: sleep, workout, eat, sleep, play cards, bullshit, and sleep some more.

For the whole first week that I was back, they gave us apples on our breakfast trays. This was rare, so the apples were highly coveted and could be used for more than just eating.

My friend Cristie was the pod cleaner and had access to all the supplies. She came into the pod one apple day and started asking everyone for their bread and fruit. Everyone obliged, throwing their apples and breakfast bread into the garbage bag. When she asked me for the apple, I glared at her and wouldn't budge. She whispered in my ear that she was using it to make hooch, and I changed my tone entirely.

A few days passed, and I was assigned a court date. I had been in D8 for 15 days without hearing from a judge. When my name was called on the docket, I heard choirs of angels singing. I knew I'd be out soon; I could just feel it.

My court case for absconding probation was set for 8:30

the following morning. I woke up early, trying to make myself presentable. I didn't wear makeup on the outside, but jail has a way of making you feel inadequate, so I quickly brushed my teeth and dabbed a drop of extra toothpaste on a piece of paper. I began vigorously coloring with a lead pencil to create some blackness I could mix with the toothpaste. I used another toothbrush to apply the paste thinly to my eyelashes, making it look like mascara. Then, I used a pinkish-colored pencil to make more paste to put on my pale, crusty lips as lip gloss. This was about as ready as I'd ever be.

They transferred me and another group of D-block girls down to the main holding cell of the jail. They called us out one by one, cuffed our arms and legs to one another, and told us to walk out to the county van to be bussed to circuit court.

Circuit court is where they hear all the felony cases that get bonded out of district. This was where the serious cases went. There were over 15 judges practicing at this level, and I was lucky enough to get the same judge twice, so she knew my record and some of my history with the law, which automatically looked bad.

My case was set to be heard at 8:30 a.m. I watched as the other girls and guys were called out of the birdcage in the back of the courtroom to appear before the judge. I spoke with other girls about my case, and they assured me I shouldn't be getting more than 30 days with time served. Hours passed, and it was now close to lunchtime. I began to worry why my case hadn't been called yet.

At about 1:15 p.m., my case was the last one called. I looked out into the audience to see Kelly sleeping on one of the benches. At this point, I knew she was doing drugs again. There was one man sitting behind her who didn't speak to her, so I assumed he didn't know Kelly.

When they called me to the front to approach the bench, my judge just lit into me. I didn't even have time to speak before she banged the gavel and sentenced me to six months. I looked at Kelly, who had started wailing and crying in the courtroom as she was walking out with this gentleman.

I remember feeling angry with her, thinking the judge saw her nodding off and knew she was using again and wouldn't let me go back to that. Judge Druzinski then told me if I completed a course called CRP while in jail, I'd be eligible for early release.

At that moment, I had no idea just how much my life was about to change forever. The only time it's acceptable to cry in jail is after sentencing, and even then, you have to be careful about who you confide in.

On the van ride back, I was talking with a girl who asked how much time I was just sentenced to. I began to tear up as I told her, "Six months."

This girl was an accessory to a murder and a burglary that had gone wrong and was facing 20 years to life. When I told her my fate, she grew irritated and said she would pray to get only six months and that I should be grateful.

Grateful? Grateful that I got time? Okay, bitch. You're just the wrong person to talk to. Who in their right mind would be grateful for any kind of sentence?

As I made it back to jail and into D8, I quickly ran to Cristie to ask her about the hooch. All I knew was that I could really use a drink at that moment.

"It will probably be ready tomorrow, and you get the first sip, Chelzzz. I got you always," Cristie replied. So I laid in bed, thinking about what my life had become and who I would be in six months, and wept under a blanket, alone.

"GET UP, LADIES! LEAVE EVERYTHING ON YOUR BEDS. SHAKE DOWN, LADIES!"

I was awoken the next morning by the deputies, yelling as they entered our cells, picking up our mats and commissary bins, and throwing everything around the room.

My eyes locked onto Cristie's as she tried to push her bin under the bed and cover it with a blanket. She kicked it a little, but it didn't budge. When no one was looking, she gave it another kick, and we all heard a giant POP!

The room began to reek of stale bread and apple slices. The odor was pungent and filled the air quickly. The hooch had exploded all over two of the deputies and the floor. We all sat in silence as they screamed and demanded to know who was making the wine. "Henson! This has your name all over it! You're going to Max!"

As I got up to pack the small amount of belongings I had, Cristie jumped out of her bed. "I did it," she said. "It wasn't Chelzzz."

I was shocked. This was all of our fault, and she was about to do a few months in lockdown for this. But Cristie just looked at me and said, "I told you I always got your back."

In the days that followed, I was classified into "A pod" and moved upstairs into general population. I now had my own one-person cell, with a desk and a small window where I could just barely see the city life bustling outside through the tiny crack in the concrete.

Being a part of that world felt so far away, and the feelings of despair set in as I thought about the months I had left. At first, I spent my time like I had every other time I had been locked up, but the conversations with other inmates left me feeling anxious and unfulfilled. I wondered what I could do in there to still have some sense of purpose in life.

Kelly visited me twice a week, putting money on the phone and $20 in my commissary account for the week. It didn't buy much, and I was cold and hungry on a daily basis. More than my physical starvation, I felt emotionally and spiritually starved as well. I was no longer interested in discussing dreams of what I would do when I got out with the other inmates. I began isolating myself, spending my days reading and working out.

I pushed myself in my CRP class to get everything I could out of it so I wouldn't end up back in jail. Something clicked, and I realized I could either waste six months of my life or make sure I was never in this situation again. I chose the latter.

About a month in, a deputy gave me the book *The Purpose Driven Life*, which put a lot of things into perspective for me.

For months, until I was released, Kelly and I talked on the phone about what we would do differently when I got out. I clung to those conversations, needing to believe every word she said. But while I was growing inside, she remained stagnant, and I didn't realize I was outgrowing her until I was released and found she was still the same person she was before I went in. But I wasn't. I had transformed, and I was ready to embrace my new lifestyle, even if it meant losing her or part of her in the process.

For the first time in my life, I felt a sense of self-worth, and I wasn't going to let our old behaviors get in the way of that.

At least, that's what I hoped for. That's what I was striving for. In jail, I did a lot of reading that guided me spiritually through tough times. I was able to start identifying my purpose—what I liked doing, what I wanted to do when I got out, and how I wanted to be in the next several years. I was ultimately able to see beyond today to realize that I, too, possessed a light inside me that could bless others. I no longer had to be the person I was yesterday.

This newfound sense of freedom, even while incarcerated, had me plotting and planning for different purposes. By brushing up on skills through books, I felt confident that after jail, I could land some kind of job. I was putting in as much work as I could in the space I was in. Seeing that others were only there to pass the time, not interested in truly growing, I began withdrawing from them. Separating myself from the crowd felt very foreign, and I spent a lot of time feeling lonely. But conversations with others who weren't being spiritually moved actually exhausted me mentally. I was no longer the same person who entered jail in handcuffs. Even though I was still incarcerated, I was free from myself.

I was blessed to have had that time in jail. I'm sure most people will read that and think I'm crazy, but that's where God was able to reach me most directly. I had the willingness to change, but I was still devoted to Kelly, and that conflicted with my spiritual journey. A negative connection of any kind that can jeopardize your sobriety and self-discovery is called a "reservation."

I stayed on course through the rest of my jail stay and talked in detail with Kelly about creating a better life. I told her we were moving to Florida when I got out because if we ever had to be homeless again, we could sleep on the beach. But the real reason was that I desperately needed to get us both away from toxic places and faces. I needed to run as fast as I could from the people who enabled or triggered me in any way. Unfortunately, at the time, I didn't realize that Kelly was not only my biggest trigger but also my biggest reservation.

Chapter 10

The Escape Plan

About two weeks before I graduated from CRP, I was moved back down to D block for getting into a fight and sagging my pants like a thug. A few weeks earlier, a creepy deputy who ran the trustee section of the women's jail had offered me the chance to become a jail trustee. A trustee is an inmate with special privileges. They get to work for the jail for pennies an hour and can pick from the commissary bin each week for their assistance. I wasn't interested in working for free, so I politely declined.

Since I told him no, he had it out for me and made sure the remainder of my time was as uncomfortable as possible, sticking me back in D block.

The day I completed my CRP class, I knew I was eligible to go home. I began packing up the small number of items I had to my name and giving away the things I wouldn't need in the real world.

My CRP instructor called me out of the pod after my last class. She didn't have her usual happy and excited look on her face. In fact, when I approached her desk, she looked concerned and worried.

"Chelsea, during your time at MCJ, the Chesterfield police, and the Clinton Township police have been building a case against you for the home invasion involving several stolen items, including jewelry and a printer, as well as three counts of delivering and manufacturing a controlled substance to the Clinton Township police."

All I could think to myself was, "Here we go again!"

At this rate, I'd never be getting out of jail.

My instructor informed me I would be going up in front of the judge for all these pending cases early the next morning and let me know she had written a letter advocating for my release.

I tried to go back to my cell to get some sleep. I tossed and turned, crying on and off, trying to muster up a little faith. The Lord had gotten me through this far. I had to believe that whatever happened, I would be okay.

I had been locked up for over four months now, and all I wanted was to get out and get a job so I could save money to leave Michigan permanently.

I had outgrown this lawless town and was in search of a more structured way of life. I didn't know how I was going to make it happen, but I knew there was no going back.

I was awakened the next morning by a deputy calling me for court. I had been lying in my bunk for hours waiting on that call. I was ready—or at least as ready as I could ever be. Nervous and sleepy, I marched my way down the hall to the room where they conduct video court. To my surprise, I was called up to the bench right away. The judge read out the letter that my circuit court judge and my CRP instructor had written to him. I started tearing up when they expressed how much I had changed and that they thought it would be best for me to be released on my own recognizance.

The first judge agreed to "time served" and said that if the other court judge agreed, I could be going home that afternoon.

I had back-to-back court sessions, and the second judge said the same thing. I could be released on bond and would need to come back to court at a later date to be sentenced.

This was a good sign that I would likely be placed on probation and could avoid further jail time as long as I kept my nose clean.

I walked back to D block and called Kelly to tell her I was being released. She sounded off, but I didn't care. All I could think of was taking a real shower, going to the dentist, and eating McDonald's.

For the first time in four months, I was able to take a deep breath.

"HENSON, PACK IT UP; YOU'RE OUTTA HERE!" Action Amy, the Barbie-looking deputy, called my name to leave.

"Can you believe I'm finally out of here!" I exclaimed sarcastically.

"Let's just hope it's not another revolving door for you, Henson. You've been in here every other week for the past year," Amy replied.

I laughed and ran out as fast as I could, threw my tan uniforms in the bin, kicked off my Jesus shoes, and grabbed my black Jordan Spizikes, a white tee, a pair of clean boxers, and the gray and black sweatpants from my property bin.

Kelly was waiting in the lobby when I arrived. Those final

moments, when you see each other, but the glass door is still separating you from your loved ones and freedom, were the jail's way of having one last sick joke at your expense.

As the glass door slid open, I pried it wider with my arm and slipped through. "Hands off the door, Henson, or you're getting locked back up," a guard warned, but I ignored them and made it through the sally port as a free man.

Kelly greeted me with a long kiss and a change of clothes. This time, I wasn't feeling sexual. I just wanted to get the hell out of Dodge before they realized they'd made a mistake by letting me out in the first place. I changed quickly and asked Kelly about our game plan. She told me she had a van for us and could get us a hotel room for one night. After that, we would have to stay with the owner of the van at his dad's place, but "Don't worry, his dad is never home."

This sounded sketchy to me. Everything seemed sketchy as I walked into the gray, overcast day outside the jail. I smelled the gas and oil-stained air and heard people and cars bustling around me, but I didn't feel like I was part of this life I had just walked back into. Not to mention, I had been gone for four months and was walking right back into the same situation.

I stared into Kelly's eyes. They looked tired, drained, and pinned out. I knew at that moment she had been doing heroin the entire time I was in jail. I saw the scars on her forearm where she had been shooting up, and my heart sank. I wasn't there to protect her. I couldn't save her.

At that moment, I felt 100 percent alone, and didn't realize how far gone she was.

Kelly told the owner of the van, a young guy named Abe, that I would be driving.

Driving? Me? It had been four months since I'd even looked at a car, and I still didn't have a license. But reluctantly, I got into the driver's seat while Abe sat in the back.

We drove to the Comfort Inn, and all I could think about was Jhene Aiko's song, "Comfort Inn Freestyle," where the relationship ended one night at a Comfort Inn. I pondered the sad irony that was now my life.

When we arrived and got to our room, Kelly pulled out a small box and presented it to me as we sat on the bed.

As I opened the package, I was shocked to see Xanax pills, Suboxone, weed pre-rolled by her, Adderall, and other scattered pills inside the small container.

"Kelly," I said nervously, "I have to go to court in two days. They're going to drug test me."

"Well, weed was already in your system, so we can at least smoke," she replied, slightly annoyed.

So, like a true codependent, I agreed and smoked. As the smoke filled my lungs, I became high and paranoid. With each puff, I felt my guilt increasing as anxiety and fatigue crept in. The disappointment in myself settled in, and the feeling of loneliness returned to my soul.

As Kelly tried to cuddle me, I felt myself grow stiff and rigid. Her once comforting touch now felt like the stroke of an enemy.

I lay in bed, pretending to sleep. Pretending to be okay. Pretending to understand. I lay there, pretending to exist, falling asleep and praying that this was all just a dream.

The next day, we arrived at Abe's father's house. It was a beautiful, large home in the middle of nowhere, with very little furniture, food, or any true indication that anyone lived there. Here I was, stuck in the suburbs, once again a sitting duck.

I called my attorney to ask when she would be arriving for my court date. I was placed on hold while the secretary gathered her notes on my case. Upon leaving Macomb County Jail, my mother felt guilty about me being locked up and gave my attorney $500 to pay the restitution for the items I had stolen when I robbed my roommate's house.

The secretary got back on the phone and told me that Jenna, my attorney, had withdrawn from the case and that my court date was scheduled for 8 a.m. that morning. I had already missed it... I was now right back in the same situation I had been in before I got locked up.

I informed Kelly, who didn't seem to care. She told me that she and Abe needed to run out for something and said, "Just stay here" at this stranger's house by myself until they got back. I knew Kelly and Abe were going to get dope. Abe had talked about it the night before with very little attempt to hide his excitement. Kelly lied, saying she was getting it for him but wasn't using it herself. I knew this was a facade, but she was all I had. If I started a fight with her over the dope, I risked having to move forward in life alone, and I was much too codependent to risk losing her.

At the time, Kelly and I only had one cell phone because she had sold mine for drugs while I was locked up. She took the phone with her, so I was literally stranded at this stranger's house with no vehicle, no phone, and no cable.

I sat in his guest room, staring at the wall for what seemed like hours before they returned. When they arrived, Kelly was noticeably messed up and whispering something in Abe's ear as I walked down the steps.

This infuriated me, and I couldn't take it anymore. I got in both their faces and started a huge argument. I slapped Abe across his stoned face and grabbed Kelly by the arm.

Because of my actions, Abe didn't want us to stay there anymore, so I called my mom to explain the situation. She reluctantly allowed Kelly and me to stay with her.

I was motivated and wanted to get things right quickly so we could leave town. Running was going to be my only option. I didn't have the money to hire new attorneys, and I risked going back to jail for many years if I showed up to court. Kelly and I decided we would work hard for a few months, save up, and move to Florida. My reasoning was if I was going to be homeless, at least I'd be somewhere warm.

My mother's house was never a permanent solution, especially after I was locked up for stealing from her. I always had a hint of guilt and a feeling that I was being watched when I visited.

Nonetheless, it was my only option for the time being, and certainly more comfortable than Abe's place.

I found work easily once I was back at my mom's. An old sponsor of mine owned a cleaning company that needed extra help. Kelly and I began cleaning commercial warehouses during the day to save up for our big move.

I was still in contact with Bre's mom, selling her Adderall now and again. She mentioned she had a van for sale that I could have for a month's script of Adderall. I was excited. We needed wheels if we wanted to make it to Florida, so it felt like we were one step in the right direction.

Bre's mom failed to tell me until we got there that the van had a dirty title, and I couldn't get it transferred. At this point, I didn't care; we just needed a car. I gave her the paper prescription, which I had not yet gotten filled, and drove away.

That evening, Kelly and I wanted some onion chips from the gas station up the street. We hopped in the van and began our quick journey to the store for snacks. As I turned onto the overpass, a cop got behind me and flicked his lights. Here we go again... I waited until he was out of his car and approaching the window. Before I could even think, my foot hit the gas, flooring it through the red light and onto the expressway. I sped along the shoulder as fast as I could, exited a few miles up, and pulled into a subdivision where I ditched the car and started walking on foot to the nearest store. Kelly and I called for a ride and got out of there before the police could catch us. That was close... *way too close.*

The next day, I called Bre's mom to complain about what had happened. Although it wasn't her fault, I didn't feel comfortable giving the van another try. Being the back-handed criminal I was, I voided the script I sold her by calling the doctor and claiming it was stolen. I was then able to get the script myself and resell it. We were now up $600, but we still had no car...

While I was locked up, Kelly had really blown up my social media accounts. A lot of new eyes were on me, and many local people started listening to my music. I was approached by a young artist who wanted a feature and offered to pay me $1,000 for my verse. This was the money Kelly and I needed for our move, so I jumped on the opportunity. The next week, we recorded the song. We were now up $1,600, but we still needed a car.

I reached out to a friend who owned a dealership, and he offered us one of his beat-up SUVs for $600 down. I happily accepted the offer, and Kelly and I went to his shop to fill out the paperwork and take home our new, used beater.

Everything went as planned, and Kelly and I drove off

the lot. We couldn't have gotten further than a block before another cop was behind me. This time, before he could flick his lights, I pulled down a side street, parked the car, and got out. The cop circled the block a few times before driving away. That's when Kelly and I hopped back in the car and started driving—and didn't stop. I had no idea I was driving into a life I could never have imagined.

Chapter 11
Moonlight and Meltdowns

The drive to Florida was stressful and long. Neither of us had a license, and Kelly was a horrible driver, so I was stuck driving the 21 hours from Detroit to Miami alone. Kelly played DJ, which I always hated because she liked the corniest rap songs, but I managed to tune out the music and her chatter and daydream about the new life we were about to begin.

We made our way to the South with only $1,000 and a dream. Our thought process was that if we were going to be homeless, at least we would be in a warm climate.

We stopped at a few cheap motels on the way down before we finally hit the tip of Florida's coastline late on February 14, 2016. When we reached Cocoa Beach, I pulled off at a Motel 6 right on the water. Before checking into the room, Kelly and I ran to the beach and fell into the freezing cold, salty waves. Tears filled my eyes as I gasped for breath with the waves crashing into my face. We fell into the sand, holding each other, peeling off our wet clothes, and kissing as the waves crashed between our legs. We made love passionately under the moonlight in the warm winter air. For the first time in months, I felt we were truly reconnected.

Kelly and I dressed back into our wet clothes and headed to the front desk of Motel 6 to get a room for the night. Our goal was always Miami, but we didn't have a solid plan, so we rested our heads for the night and woke up early to figure out the next steps. Without a clear destination, we just drove until we reached Broward County, about 10 minutes north of Fort Lauderdale. We found a room for rent, priced at $110 per week, and settled into a chopped-up condo in a 55-plus community that was just a block from the beach.

The night we arrived, we had dinner at a nice little diner by the house, where I filled out a job application. They interviewed me on the spot and hired me, so the next day, I started waitressing at Lester's. I was working six days a week and making great money. We were finally in a decent position. Because of this, Kelly and I were looking to upgrade our living situation and began packing the car to the brim with stolen appliances and household items taken from the condo we were renting. Our car (already an eyesore in South Florida) was packed to capacity with all of our newfound treasures.

On one of my days off, Kelly and I decided we wanted a lemonade from Chick-fil-A. With the car full to the brim, we headed the short distance to the drive-through. As I was turning into the parking lot, a police officer pulled up next to us, and we made eye contact. I must have looked nervous and suspicious because they turned on their signal, got behind me, and flashed their lights. I quickly parked the car, hoping the officer would leave, but he didn't. He approached the vehicle, and I explained that we were visiting from out of town, just stopping for a lemonade. He questioned why the car was so packed, and neither Kelly nor I had an answer. I told him I left my license at home and gave him a fake name. This was it—I had no way out. I was caught red-handed. I had multiple felony warrants out for my arrest in Michigan, and I was surely going to be extradited back to serve a prison sentence if I didn't act quickly.

I looked at Kelly as the officer went back to his squad car to run my name. I jumped through the passenger-side door, unnoticed, and made a run for it. I was wearing a bright yellow cut-off shirt, which I ripped off and threw in the opposite direction of where I was running. I kicked off my flip-flops and ran shirtless and barefoot toward the nearest exit. The Chick-fil-A was in a plaza with shopping centers and a movie theater. I pushed through a crowd of people, trying to blend in despite my lack of shoes or a shirt.

I made it to the back of the building, where I was faced with a giant brick wall. Somehow, I scaled the wall like Spider-Man, jumped down, and kept running through a neighborhood.

After a few blocks, I saw a large bush covering part of a side street. It was big enough for me to hide in while still being able to see what was happening on the street. I heard sirens—multiple sirens. I was shaking, sweating, and almost out of breath. A cop car was circling the neighborhood, and all I could think was that I was screwed.

I stayed hidden in the bush for what felt like hours until

I heard Kelly's voice. "Baby, baby, where are you?" she whispered as she walked.

"HERE! I'M IN THE BUSH!" I whispered back.

"What should I do?" Kelly asked.

"Are they gone?" I replied.

"They impounded the car and let me go, but they're still looking for you."

"Okay," I said calmly. "Call a cab, walk around the block until it comes, give them the nearest house address, and get out of here until the ride shows up."

"Okay, babe, but..." Kelly started to reply.

"BUT NOTHING!" I quickly cut her off with a whisper scream. "JUST DO IT AND STOP TALKING TO A BUSH; YOU'RE GOING TO GET ME CAUGHT!"

I waited what felt like hours for the cab driver to pull up. Before Kelly could even speak, I hopped into the back of the cab and put my head down on her lap. I couldn't risk having the feds see my face. We headed back home, where the cops were circling the block. They had found our address and other personal information by searching the vehicle I had abandoned.

We managed to get in, gather the rest of our belongings, and get the hell out of Dodge before anyone noticed. We stayed at a cheap dope motel called the Cumberland in a more mainland area of Broward County and paid for a two-week stay.

This tapped out most of our savings, and I was eager to get back to Lester's for my next shift since we really needed the money. When I got to work, I was met with a disappointed glance and was told the supervisor needed to speak with me. Since I was the last one hired and it was no longer the busy season, things were slowing down, and he needed to lay me off for the time being. I was devastated and unsure of what to do next. Without this job, Kelly and I couldn't even afford to eat. If it weren't for my free meals while working there, we would've been in serious trouble, and now we were exactly that.

Moving to the dope motel was difficult for Kelly. Seeing the dirty syringes in the parking lot and constantly being approached with "Are you good?" made life even harder. On top of that, Kelly and I couldn't even afford any weed, which was the only thing that seemed to give her any kind of joy.

I found work a few blocks away at a vacation sales company, and Kelly spent her days at home, uninterested in finding work, even though we really needed two incomes. Kelly turned to social media for assistance, asking random people on Facebook to wire us money. I had to admit that it worked for her. She was so pretty that she had no problem getting a few people to send a hundred bucks here and there. But this wasn't enough to get her the weed she craved, so she turned to another app that connected stoners for smoke sessions.

We met a few guys and girls through the app who came over and smoked with us. One evening, a nice guy named Gus came to the hotel from Palm Beach County to hang out. He took us to get food and empathized with us about our situation. Gus never wanted anything more than friendship, and he offered to let us stay with him rent-free until we got on our feet. If it wasn't for Gus, I wouldn't be where I am today. I owe a lot of my success in Florida to his kindness.

Kelly and I stayed with Gus for five months until we were finally stable enough to move into our own place. The place wasn't much to brag about—we were back in the hood, paying triple the rent—but I was proud of myself for doing it all on my own.

Kelly still hadn't found a job, but she took it upon herself to start growing my social media around my music and marketing my songs in all her free time. In a matter of two years, Kelly had built up my social media and was booking me steady shows across the U.S., traveling out of state almost every weekend.

I was able to find steady employment with a great sales organization and quickly rose through the ranks, becoming the company's vice president in just three years. At 22 years old, I went from an unemployable felon to the star salesperson of my organization, making over six figures a year.

When the money really started coming in, I realized there were many areas of my past life that needed to be cleaned up in order for me to live to my full potential. I came clean to my boss about my priors and the pending cases back in Michigan, and I began the process to redeem myself.

I hired a great criminal defense attorney and started drug testing to show that I could comply with probation. I traveled back to Michigan for multiple court dates until the cases were finally resolved. Many months and thousands of dollars later, I was placed on probation for one year and allowed to reside in Florida during that time. I guess it's safe to say that when you do the next right thing, no matter what, God blesses you immensely.

I have yet to fully grasp how to heal from the codependent abuse I received as a child, but today I'm aware of it. In my mid-20s, upon moving to Florida, I worked incredibly hard and became extremely successful. I rose to VP of my company in just two short years, making me the youngest person in my organization with a leadership role. My music took off, and I began performing monthly all over the United States, living the dream from an outsider's perspective. However, my perfectionism constantly left me feeling unfulfilled, as if I didn't quite make the mark. I became a miserable workaholic, hating myself for not being perfect and unable to enjoy the success I created.

In March 2019, Kelly and I curated an amazingly successful show on the main street during the SXSW Festival. Over 3,000 people celebrated my 26th birthday and watched me perform live during the biggest showcase of the year. I met with various organizations and panels of A&R reps that could help push me in the right direction. I had the best week of my life, and I was flying high.

As things settled back down, we returned home, and I got back to my duties at my 9-to-5 job. A few days passed, and I was fully back into the swing of things.

It was a Tuesday morning like any other. I was plugging away at my computer, making the next sale, when my personal cell phone rang. My Aunt Barb was calling me, and this was odd—we hadn't really spoken in a while. If we did talk, it was usually through my mom, so it was abnormal for her to call me directly.

I stepped into the hallway to answer the call. Her weak voice indicated that she had been crying. "Chels, you need to come home—your mom's cancer is spreading, and it's getting bad."

I paused, not understanding. "What do you mean, her cancer?" I asked, stunned. "My mom has cancer?"

"You mean no one told you?!" my aunt exclaimed.

"Chelsea, you need to come home now! She's blind, it's spread to her brain, and the doctors don't even know where it's coming from. Get home, Chelsea!"

At that moment, I didn't even think—I was on autopilot. All I knew was that I needed to be on the next flight to Detroit to see my mom. I packed enough clothes for a month, not knowing how long I'd be there, and headed out.

When I touched down in Detroit, I got an Uber straight to the hospital to see my mom. She was weak, speaking softly, and cried tears of joy when she heard my voice. She was able to make out shapes and colors and recognized me by my bright red hair as I sat beside her in the hospital bed.

I spent hours there until I was so fatigued I could barely keep my eyes open. For days, my mother would call me in the middle of the night, begging for me to come to her rescue, telling me she was scared and didn't want to sleep alone in the hospital. It broke my heart to hear my mom cry in fear for her own safety. She was so medicated that she was only somewhat aware of what was actually happening to her.

Days passed, and the hospital staff began discussing alternate options. At this point, my mother's cancer was stage 4, and they had determined it was coming from her pancreas. She had no chance of survival. The words echoed in my ear without fully resonating. All I wanted was to keep my mom comfortable. I regretfully had to return to Florida for a couple of days to get my affairs in order, bring my pets to Michigan, and arrange for my car to be transported. When I returned, my mother had worsened. Once again, I bee-lined straight for the hospital upon arrival. My mom was excited because she knew she was going home, but she kept asking if I was taking her to the beach. More than anything, she wanted to spend her final days in Florida with me in the warmth and sunlight.

My mother was transferred to hospice, and I was setting up my childhood home so that I could better care for her upon her arrival. All she wanted was to be with me. She wanted so badly to come down to Florida and live the rest of her days in the sun on the beach. We couldn't get her there, so I tried my best to make her as comfortable as possible at home. I held my mom's hand as she was taken in an ambulance and transported to the house. All the necessary equipment was delivered as she arrived, and we worked to get her set up and comfortable in her bedroom.

Her room no longer looked like the bedroom I remembered from my childhood. Her bed and various antiques had been moved out to create more space and reduce clutter for easier maneuvering. In their place were an oxygen tank, a small twin hospital bed, IV bags, and a commode. It made me sick to my stomach to see her warm, cozy bedroom become so sterile and uninviting.

The first night was difficult, to say the least. I used baby monitors to listen in case my mom woke up. The monitors crackled loudly that first night. I woke up exhausted to find my mother sitting up in bed, trying to use the commode on her own. She didn't make it and had an accident. I started cleaning her off, quietly crying to myself. My mom was calling me her sister's name, unaware of where she was or what was going on. I knew then that things had taken a drastic turn for the worse.

The next day, I told my father about the difficulties I had experienced the night before, and he suggested it was time to put the Depends on her. After changing her sheets three separate times the previous night, I reluctantly agreed. My mom fought us, kicking and grunting, refusing to wear them. My dad helped me change her and get her ready for the day. That morning, many visitors came, and my mom was talking as best she could, but by the afternoon, she was worn out.

My mom had so much faith up until the moment she died. She knew she would be okay, even though she was leaving behind a group of broken and confused loved ones. She asked me to play songs by Lauren Daigle, and she would lift her frail arms to the heavens to praise her Creator, even through her grueling pain. She still loved the Lord through her blindness and sickness, and if she could have literal blind faith in her weakest hour, the least I could do was reciprocate that.

I'll never forgive my father for failing to tell me my mother was sick sooner. They had been divorced for years, and while I thanked him for stepping up, a part of me saw his greed. I will never forget that he took most of my mother's assets and misplaced her family heirloom teapot, which had been passed down for generations. I didn't want to rock the boat because he was the only parent I had left, so I never expressed how hurt I was by the way he handled my mother's death. Even the cards given to him for the funeral, which he didn't pay for, went toward his desires rather than being donated to the charity my mother had chosen.

The day my mom died, she seemed to be doing a little better. She had visitors in and out all day, but by evening, she was too weak to even swallow. As I sat alone with her, holding her hand and brushing her hair with my fingertips, I noticed she hadn't swallowed the last dose of liquid medication I gave her. The afternoon dose was still sitting under her tongue, mixed with saliva. Her breathing was faint and far apart, and I knew the time had come. I called Kelly and my father into the room, and they stood by the door, giving me space. I kissed my mother and whispered in her ear, "It's okay, Mom, let go." Laying in my arms, just after I uttered those words, my mother took her last breath.

Grief blindsided me in a painfully familiar way. While planning her funeral, I started drinking every night to numb the pain. It took me two weeks to get everything prepared, mostly because I was doing it all on my own. My mother's sisters did a lot—they came over daily to help me close out her accounts and shut down the life she had built. They baked for the funeral and helped with picture collages, but most of the planning fell on my shoulders as I once again assumed the role of caretaker.

The morning of the funeral, around 9 a.m., my aunt from my father's side greeted me with a pint of vodka, asking if I wanted to take shots in the parking lot before the day began. A group from my father's side of the family gathered in the parking lot to pregame before the funeral, and I couldn't help but think to myself, *"This isn't normal. This isn't how you're supposed to grieve."* But I wanted to be numb, so I gave in to my need for a temporary high. We held my mother's reception lunch at the Moose Lodge, mostly so people could drink during the celebration of life. I scurried around most of the day, speaking to people and making sure everyone else was okay. I listened to stories about my mom from everyone who attended as they tried to cheer me up, reminding me of the good times. Sure, we had some good times, but a lot of my childhood was filled with pain and emptiness, and I was falling apart, confused about how I should and shouldn't feel.

That confusion made it difficult to see my mother for the person she truly was—at least for about a year. I could only speak of the good things she had to offer and the light inside her. I was afraid to say anything negative about her, stifling a lot of my own emotions to preserve her image as the woman I wanted her to be. However, as time passed, my anger and confusion festered, leaving me feeling abandoned once again and dragging me back to the shame and pain of my childhood. This made me resent my mother, allowing me to focus only on the negative things she brought to the table and the bad times I went through with her. This, in turn, fueled my shame and anger, quickly propelling me back into my addictive behaviors.

Now, my mom has been gone for almost six years. It took me about four of those years to find balance and begin to see her for who she truly was—the good and the bad. The damage and the pain she carried, which she transferred onto me. Codependency is a transferable disease.

I was blinded by my sorrow and anger, and my carried shame kept me from allowing myself to see my mother for who she was: a flawed person who made mistakes and did the best she could with what she had been taught. I had to make my own mistakes to see the pattern that needed to be broken. When I stepped back and looked at myself, I realized I was becoming my mother in all the ways I didn't want to be.

Grief is something that never truly goes away, and you have to realize there are only two ways to deal with it. You can avoid it, mask it, run from it, or self-medicate to ease the pain, but that means you're never truly healing. If you face the pain head-on, acknowledge it directly, you don't need to damage yourself in the process of healing.

I tried running for as long as I could, but I was only running in circles. When life threw me a curveball, my addiction hit a home run, blazing through all the bases and sliding back into my life like it never left. Once I realized that my addiction was my responsibility, I saw that I could use any excuse in the book to keep using. And I did—until I couldn't anymore.

Chapter 12
Behind the Smoke

The shame I carried throughout my life was ever-present, something I tried to run from for years instead of facing head-on.

Shame is taught, and when others make us feel like we have to go against our moral compass, that shame festers. I had been holding on to guilt and shame since childhood, bound by my past mistakes and the mistakes of others. I was chained to old behaviors, destined to repeat them because I hadn't yet taught myself anything different.

It wasn't until I was 30, broken and alone after yet another relapse, that I realized my past was undeniably creeping back to haunt me. This time, I had thrown away seven years of abstinence. I can't really say I was sober because I still dabbled in things I didn't consider a problem—until I created mountains of depravity so vast I couldn't see the bottom.

The world stopped as it sank in that my mom was truly gone. It hadn't fully hit me yet.

The coroners were called, and they came to take her body for cremation. The official-looking people moved around as they prepared to place my mother's body into a blue bag. With a thoughtful touch, they laid a single red rose on her hospital bed before they took her away.

I stared at the sterile room that was barely recognizable and fixated on the single rose that had replaced my mother's lifeless body.

I thought of all the nights I had spent crying in her lap, all the times we lay in bed watching our favorite shows, all the meals she cooked and things she baked during the holidays. All the times she made me feel so special.

I also thought about the times we were angry with each other during my adulthood and didn't speak for months. I felt ashamed of my younger self and wished I had realized back then how short life truly is and how precious time can be.

I grew angry with myself for the times I wasn't nurturing to her. I realize now that it was never my job to nurture my parent; it was simply a role I felt I needed to take on from a young age.

This role continued in her death as I frantically began working on her funeral arrangements, focusing all my time and energy on ensuring she had a great celebration of life. My aunts helped tremendously with dealing with her accounts and other necessary things. I hadn't been close with my mom's sisters for most of my adult life, but that changed quickly after my mother's passing. My Aunt Carol and Aunt Kathy were over every other day, helping out, cooking, cleaning, and making arrangements.

After the funeral, I stayed in Michigan for a few months but kept my place in Florida. I stayed close to my family and friends and went back to work. Kelly had begun booking me for many shows, and life kept moving.

In May of 2019, we headed back to Florida and started a large tour that covered almost 37 states. I was booked to do two or more shows per week on top of working full-time. There was no time to navigate my pain. Life was moving full speed ahead, and I didn't have the luxury of slowing down. Until I did.

In late 2019, we began to hear whispers about a new virus that was drastically affecting the nation. COVID-19 was now a daily topic on every news station. Things began shutting down, and businesses backed out of the shows we had booked. Kelly and I took a large financial loss as we had reinvested in better equipment for shows that were no longer happening.

My job was considered "essential," but my clients' jobs were not, so I essentially had no work to do, on top of no-shows to book, which left me with something I wasn't used to—an abundance of free time.

For years, I had avoided myself, my pain, my trauma, and my character defects. Now, with all this time, I was forced to sit with myself, and I realized that outside of the money and music, I didn't really like who I was.

I didn't know what needed to change to make life worth living, but now, I had the time to figure that out. As I began to see myself for who I truly was, I became highly critical. Outwardly, everything seemed okay, so I started blaming my issues on my significant other. Our fights during quarantine escalated from the typical verbal abuse to something much darker and more volatile. Things became physical, and the shame festered inside me as I hid my pain.

Chelzzz

At this point, Kelly and I were very physical. Things were being broken daily, objects thrown at each other, punches and slaps exchanged, with the ever-present threat of divorce lingering in the air. The truth was, we were both so sick and codependent that we thrived off the chaos just as much as the natural high from the good times.

With our responsibilities for work and music dwindling, I took up a new pastime—drinking. Kelly and I began day-drinking daily, often starting out happy but ending in an emotional implosion by the end of the night.

At 26 years old, I was mirroring the dysfunctional relationship I had witnessed between my parents as a child.

As things started getting back to normal, the damage we had done to each other in the relationship was irreversible and irreparable, but the bond of dysfunction and the fear of what could be kept us together far longer than we should have been.

We fought for months and continued drinking every night. It never occurred to me that the drinking was a huge part of the problem.

I was no longer day-drinking, as I had gone back to work. Venues were reopening, and we were now able to start booking shows again.

It was my mistake not to see that Kelly's drinking had become more than just a hobby—it was now a habit, much like her past heroin use.

As I got back to work full force, I expected Kelly to do the same. Weeks passed, and I still wasn't getting any show bookings. My patience with Kelly had worn thin, and I began demanding that she improve, often yelling at her until one of us snapped and we physically attacked each other.

Kelly was sipping Bacardi out of a water bottle most mornings and was drunk before I even started work. This led to more random, uncalled-for outbursts and an inability to reason with her.

Things grew more toxic, and I couldn't take it anymore. In 2021, Kelly and I split up and divorced.

I quickly realized that Kelly was only half of the problem, and I now faced a crossroads. Do I look at myself and make a change? Or do I keep ignoring the issues right in front of me that only I had the power to fix? It sounds like an easy decision, but if it were that easy, everyone would do it.

Without having to play caretaker to my emotionally damaged spouse, I felt a sense of freedom that I hadn't experienced in a long time. Kelly and I had married at 21, when I was still very much an adolescent, trying to grow alongside someone who wasn't interested in bettering herself, which left me pulling most of the weight and being the "responsible one."

As I no longer felt weighed down by my ex, I began loosening up and allowing myself to enjoy life without being so uptight all the time.

I got involved with an older woman who was friends with a few people I hung out with. It became clear early on that this was a partying group of grown women who couldn't control themselves when intoxicated. I blended right in, letting my inner wild side shine as I began taking more risks and going to extremes to make them laugh, often hurting myself in the process.

The relationship didn't work out, as most women wanted monogamy, and I wasn't interested in settling down. But I was okay with that because I had made what I thought were great friends in the process.

One of the older women in my friend group and I became platonically close. We did a lot together despite the age difference, and I truly thought she would be someone I could depend on for a long time. Brooke was wild and had her own demons, but she seemed to have her life together for the most part.

In June of that year, I decided to travel back to Michigan to spend time with my family and see Kelly. I took Brooke with me since she had never been there, and I could use some emotional support while dealing with my ex. Kelly and I had been speaking for a while, though most conversations turned into fights. Mostly, I just wanted to meet up for sex. The new fake lesbians I had been spending time with were not satisfying, and it had been a few months since I had even gotten off during sex. I'm not sure who else needs to travel out of state for a booty call, but the desperation was real.

The night we arrived, Kelly came by our Airbnb. I was instantly annoyed and remembered why I was no longer with her. She stayed the night (although, after we had sex, I tried my hardest to get her out of there). Kelly always had a way of overstaying her welcome. When she woke up the next morning, she heard Brooke and I planning activities for the day. I told her it was just going to be an "us" thing and that I'd meet up with her before I left. She was upset, as she still very much wanted to get back together, but she said okay and went home.

Brooke and I started the day with brunch and shots. We explored downtown Detroit, bar-hopping and making the most of our "Sunday Funday." As the day came to an end, Brooke asked if we could take the long way home, driving through the ghetto so she could really see the city of Detroit.

I drove down the decrepit streets of Gratiot, showing her the decay that I was formed from. She looked with wide eyes at the abandoned city that held a secret life she could never understand.

I noticed that we had been riding on E for a while, so I decided to stop for gas. As I was filling up, a homeless-looking man approached my vehicle. I drunkenly started chatting with him and asked if he could get me some crack. At this point, I hadn't fully plunged back into my addiction. I was drinking heavily, but I had yet to venture into harder drugs.

Brooke overheard the conversation and became nervous. I continued filling up the tank as she got into the driver's seat of my Ford Flex. I shook off the gas nozzle and grabbed onto the passenger-side door, arguing with Brooke to get out of the driver's seat. Before I could finish my sentence, my legs were whipped from under me, and the car sped down the road, dragging my body along with it. I couldn't let go because if I did, I would have been hit by oncoming traffic. I had to hold on for four blocks until she ran a red light, and I could finally free myself.

When I came to, the police and paramedics were already at the scene. Bystanders had called the cops to my rescue. As they tried to backboard me, concerned that I had a spinal injury, I jumped up and started screaming about my car being stolen.

I refused medical care, and the police drove me to my father's house, as they could only take me within city limits. When I arrived, I began hysterically explaining what had happened. My dad was furious on my behalf—always on my side, no matter who was right or wrong. We hopped in his truck and headed to my Airbnb. On the way, Brooke sent me a photo of my dog, Mia, with her on the porch of the Airbnb, along with a text saying, *"Where are you?"* Was she so blackout drunk that she didn't realize what had just happened?

I couldn't deal with this bitch... that text *set me off*. As we pulled up to the house, I saw my car in the driveway. I limped into the Airbnb with crazy, drunken strength. When I arrived, I got in Brooke's face and threatened her until she called the cops. When the new set of officers arrived, I was the only one with visible injuries, so Brooke was taken into custody. At the time, I didn't realize the extent of my injuries, so I decided not to press charges.

The next day, I tried to get out of bed but collapsed onto the floor. My knees were the size of grapefruits, swollen and covered in cuts and bruises. I called my father for help getting to the hospital. Being out of state, my insurance didn't cover much, and there was very little I could do.

I couldn't walk, so I asked Kelly to come back to the Airbnb to help me for a few days. She kept saying, "If I was with you, that would have never happened." After struggling with frustration and pain for days, it was finally time to head back home. Due to my injuries, my dad had to take off work, drive my car back down to Florida, and stay with me for a while to take care of me.

It was a long and uncomfortable road of physical therapy, but I was finally able to walk again and get back to my daily activities.

You'd think that after such a traumatic experience, I would have seen that my addiction was becoming a major problem in my life. However, because I was quite literally the victim in this situation, I was unable to see my role in it and continued to blame the people around me for the outcomes. Thus, I kept re-creating the same experiences in different ways, with different people, expecting a different result. I was a delusional codependent, operating on pure insanity.

Everything in me was screaming for me to take a break from dating and begin a journey of self-discovery. Unfortunately, my codependent nature was too strong to believe I could thrive alone, so I sought out validation from yet another person.

I'm not sure what made Allison different from the other women I had been with. She had a smile that could light up a room, with the most captivating mix of forest green and ice blue eyes and the cutest little freckles. She carried herself with poise and grace—Allison was the epitome of class, which was not something I typically attracted.

Most of my exes struggled with addiction issues, incredibly low self-esteem, and baggage that clung to them like dark clouds, ever-present and ready to rain down at any moment.

Allison, however, could hold a conversation and challenge my thought process. She was educated and articulate, a combination I had never experienced before. In fact, the girl I briefly dated before meeting Allison didn't even speak English, and we communicated solely through a translator app.

Allison and I quickly bonded over the trauma of our deceased parents and began leaning on each other for support, love, and encouragement. She moved into my house, and I started pulling out all the stops to "wow" my new girlfriend.

We partied a lot when we first got together, enjoying lavish nights out at expensive nightclubs, dinners catered by private chefs, and splurging on designer clothes and five-star vacations. I was quickly burning through my life savings without a care in the world.

Early in our relationship, I took a work trip to NYC and flew Allison out a few days later to join me. On our last night in New York, we were out bar-hopping, enjoying the bustling atmosphere around us. We stumbled into a strip club and got a section. We sat there drinking, laughing, and tipping the dancers when a girl pulled us aside and asked if we wanted to try some cocaine. Without a second thought, we both started doing lines in the bathroom stall. Most of what happened after that was a blur.

I woke up frantically trying to piece together the events of the night before, realizing we had overslept, missed our flight, and overstayed our checkout time. Panic set in as I acknowledged my irresponsibility, and all I wanted to do was cry. I shamefully called my boss to tell him I had messed up and asked for help with changing our flight and booking another night at the hotel. At this point, you'd think I would have learned my lesson, but the guilt consumed me, and I stood at a crossroads. My active addiction was taking control, and I had to decide: admit the mistake and move forward, or become the mistake and plunge deeper into the dark and ever-so-familiar rabbit hole.

As Allison and I finally headed home from New York, I was hungover and depressed. The guilt from screwing up weighed heavily on me. As we approached JFK airport, a large pit formed in my stomach. I wanted to run away from the wreckage I was creating, but I knew I couldn't do that without running straight into the chaos.

I've always struggled with guilt. For me, guilt is a far worse punisher than anyone's harsh words or criticism. So once again, I stood at a crossroads. I could either accept my mistake and move forward—after all, nothing but my ego had been bruised thus far—or take the path I usually traveled and plunge into utter self-destruction as a way to get back at myself and avoid the reality that I was solely responsible for creating.

As we checked our bags and walked through security, the answer seemed clear: I needed to get home and get back on track. However, the pain from my hangover, along with my emotional distress, was screaming for a quick and easy fix. My addict brain had kicked in, and I was running on autopilot. Without thinking, I suggested we pass the hour and wait for our flight by drinking at a bar near our gate.

I ordered two double shots of Casamigos Reposado for Allison and me. I slammed the first shot without a second thought, and the pain began to ease. My anxiety started to quiet as I reached for the second glass. I inhaled the sweet vanilla aroma of the tequila and sipped slowly. Before I knew it, there were at least ten empty glasses in front of me, and it was time to board our flight.

I was now happily wasted. I asked the bartender for a to-go cup and got six straight shots of tequila to sip on during the flight. As we boarded and took our seats, I started making jokes and flipping off the flight attendants as they made announcements. A few moments later, several JetBlue flight attendants approached us and asked us to deplane. I caused a belligerent scene, hollering at the employees as they gathered our belongings so we could exit the aircraft.

They put us on a flight home two hours later, so naturally, the only logical thing to do was go back to the bar and drink some more. I drank myself to sleep, and we somehow made it home safely without any more detours or interruptions.

Once we got back to Florida, the party never really stopped. I had awakened something inside me that had been dormant for a long time. My addiction had returned with a vengeance. It felt like I picked up right where I had left off, and the voices in my head were just as diabolical as ever.

"You got this."

"You're in control."

"A few drinks won't hurt."

"You're not hurting anyone by drinking."

"Everyone does coke—it's not a big deal."

"I can stop whenever I want."

The lies I told myself went on and on. Another problem emerged when I was drinking daily: I would get so drunk that I'd forget to take my bipolar meds and antidepressants. This created an elevated sense of mania that I was trying to navigate while intoxicated. The only pill I remembered to take was my Adderall, which only escalated things further, as I was literally speeding through life while constantly drunk.

The combination of Adderall and alcohol just made me want to do more coke. Weeks passed, and while I was able to hold down my job by only drinking in the afternoons and evenings, I took one or two days off work each week to indulge my impulses. We continued to spend lavishly and go out on the weekends, racking up large bills at the bars.

One night, I was tired of the horrible comedowns that came with doing too much cocaine. I recalled when I used to smoke crack and mentioned to Allison that smoking it didn't come with as bad of a comedown. Plus, I enjoyed smoking more than snorting, so I convinced her to give it a try.

I headed to a shady part of town where I bought two crack pipes and some Chore Boy. I prepared the pipes by cutting and lightly burning the Chore. We purchased about $200 worth of crack, and I began cutting the rocks into small pieces for us to smoke. I told Allison I would go first to demonstrate how it was done, but in reality, I just wanted to take that hit. My active addiction was in full force, and crack was like an old friend begging to be reacquainted. We smoked for hours, talking about deep subjects, and I felt like I was really getting to know my significant other.

This just shows how an addict's mind can twist anything into seeming like a good idea. "We were so connected, so it must be okay." The problem was that we only felt that connection the first time we smoked, and from then on, we kept chasing that same high for nearly 18 months. I was quite literally living behind a smoke screen, chasing the first thrill and trying to recreate it daily with every smoking session.

This mindset left me burning the candle at both ends in my late 20s, only to say, "Fuck it all," and start smoking crack for 18 months after a seven-year stint of abstinence.

My addiction led me to believe that, once again, I was a victim and everyone else was the problem. I truly had myself convinced that because I was still making good money and could pay my bills, I could successfully smoke crack. Let's just say that out loud one more time—I was "successfully smoking crack." What exactly does it look like to "smoke crack responsibly"? Good question—let me know if you ever find out the answer to that little riddle.

My "success" was solely defined by the amount of money I had in the bank, and when that money began running out, it became just another excuse to get high. In fact, everything became a daily excuse to hit the pipe. Even moments of excitement and joy left me feeling like I needed to celebrate with a rock. But by God, my bills were paid, so I was "successful." Meanwhile, I wanted to die on a daily basis and couldn't even look in a mirror without feeling helpless and hideous. I'm 5'7" and weighed 115 lbs. soaking wet. But I was "smoking crack successfully."

It's honestly baffling what we can convince ourselves to believe when we're avoiding our own reality. For almost two years, I lived in an abyss of loneliness and despair. I truly didn't see that I was responsible, once again, for my own depravity. If you hurt me, I would hurt myself even harder. It was a vicious cycle of narcissism and extreme loss of all self-esteem. I knew better but chose to do worse because I believed I didn't deserve better.

It took me 30 years to realize that you can reset at any time if you choose to see yourself for who you really are—a broken little kid who just needs to be loved. After all, we all have trauma from our past. Today, I choose to embrace it, change the parts I don't like, and nurture the parts I love. The reset button is always there, within our grasp, and everyone deserves a redo.

Allison knew what we were doing was wrong, and she didn't struggle with the same level of addiction as I did.

When she was ready to call it quits, I was always there to convince her to do it "one last time." That "one last time" lasted almost two years.

I had always been told that when you relapse, it takes longer each time to get back on track. I quickly learned this firsthand, as for the first time, I felt like I had no control over my life—and I was okay with it. I stuffed the pipe with another rock, flicked the lighter, and took another hit.

Chapter 13
Breaking the Cycle

Months passed, and crack became a part of our weekly activities. At first, we only smoked once or twice a week, spending a couple hundred dollars here and there. But my addiction quickly escalated to many nights a week, staying up all night and spending over $600 or more in a single day smoking crack. The conversations between us became less in-depth, and we often did our drugs and then went our separate ways. I would make music while Allison sat uncomfortably on the couch until she needed another hit. Most nights, we were so out of our minds that we ended up fighting, sometimes even physically.

It got to the point where I couldn't even look at alcohol without wanting crack instead or wanting to pair it with the alcohol. Drinking became a gateway to smoking crack.

As our relationship was crumbling, we both tried to hang on for dear life. I proposed to Allison in a very lavish way about six months into our relationship, and she said yes.

Her mom helped me plan the proposal and pick out the ring. I rented a yacht, hired a private chef, and invited her mom and aunt so they could witness me popping the question.

We had a great day and celebrated with champagne and drinks. As we sailed out and I began drinking, everything inside me wanted to smoke crack. I kept my composure until Allison and I were alone on the boat. I confided in her that I wanted to smoke, and she admitted she felt the same way.

With everything in the world to be excited about, I still wanted to celebrate with crack. That's what crack did in my life: it gave me a crutch during the bad times and heightened my experiences during the good ones. On any given day, I could come up with an excuse to use. This was new for me. Drugs in the past had helped me disconnect from life, but crack was there when I wanted to unplug from my existence or plug into it more deeply. That's why this time around was so different. I had never experienced a drug that I wanted to do even when everything was going well, a drug that I wanted to do 24/7.

When we got back home, we picked up our drugs and resumed our smoking rituals. At this point, both of us were feeling guilty, and we began blaming one another for caving into our desires.

Weeks passed, and Allison was busy planning our wedding. We were spending money left and right, and I began to get nervous as we blew through my commission checks monthly on the wedding and our habit. By then, Allison was ready to make a change. She wanted us to stop partying so much and start getting serious about our future.

I agreed because, truthfully, I wanted to stop too—but I physically couldn't.

Allison began getting rid of the liquor bottles in the house so I wouldn't be triggered. Wanting so badly to be present in our relationship, I tried my hardest to fight my daily urges. I began sneaking liquor and hiding it in my office, closing the door to sneak a few sips. This escalated to sneaking out to bars for drinks and lying about it when confronted.

I would manipulate her into caving in and smoking crack with me until she finally had enough. She moved out and told me that if I didn't go to treatment, she couldn't see a future with me. I reluctantly went to a rehab center and left after just ten days, convincing Allison that I had gotten what I needed and was a changed woman.

Two months passed while I was drying out. I was taking Xanax daily, lying about my anxiety and saying it was too high for me to cope with day-to-day life. I was just buying time until I felt like Allison was weak enough for me to convince her to smoke with me one last time. It was always "one last time"... the famous words of an addict.

One weekend, I noticed Allison was a bit restless, and I brought up smoking again. She reluctantly agreed, and we were back to the races. Even though I had stayed clean for two months, the desire had been there the whole time, and those two months of sobriety were agonizing. As I said before, I could use anything as an excuse to get high, and this time, I used Allison. I wasn't ready to make the changes I needed, so those days of sobriety weren't filled with light and the desire to better myself—they were filled with emptiness and the desire to use.

We smoked for two days in a row and fought the entire time. The last night we smoked was typical at first, but my depression and guilt consumed me, even when I was at my highest. No amount of crack could stop me from hating what I was doing to myself and Allison. That night, I decided I was done with it all. I took my gun out of the safe, closed my office door, and began loading it with bullets. I put the tip of the gun to my temple. My hand wobbled, and I pulled the trigger, but I missed and shot a bullet into the wall. A few long seconds passed before Allison burst into the room, screaming at me. All I could think was that I was such a loser that I couldn't even kill myself correctly.

I began taking Xanax, one bar after another, 4 or 5 at a time. If I couldn't die by gun, maybe the pills would work. I lost count after taking over 40 bars of Xanax. The rest of the night was a blur.

The following morning, still messed up, Allison began yelling at me to wake me up and threw something at me while I was lying in bed. In a fit of rage, I went after her, putting her in a headlock and beating her up. She called the police, and I was taken into custody.

Allison hired me an attorney and publicly canceled our wedding. I was out of my mind when they processed me, and because of the number of pills I had taken, I was placed in the mental health ward of the Broward County jail.

I've been incarcerated many times, but this time, I was terrified. I was watching mentally ill inmates behave erratically, getting a harsh, up-close look at what could be my permanent reality if I continued down this path.

When I entered the jail cell, there were several mats on the floor, and I was warned they were covered in feces. I was told to take off my shoes, so I was literally walking through someone else's piss and shit, trying to maneuver my way to the only mat left. I peeled the sticky mat off the ground and began cleaning it with toilet paper and tap water that barely trickled out of the sink. I had been to jail before, but never like this. It was obvious that most of these women in the mental health pod weren't just there for suicide attempts; they were seriously mentally ill.

I lay on my mat with my face covered by a blanket. I was so out of it from all the Xanax that I felt like this was going to be my permanent reality. Even if I was bonded out and released, I was afraid the damage I had done to my brain was too far gone, and I would forever be navigating through this fog and despair.

There was a woman locked in a separate cell facing the rest of the pod. She was about 280 lbs. and completely naked, with hair that looked like a scarecrow's—straw-like yellow and gray pieces flying in all directions. When she noticed me, she fixated on me, screaming at me through the glass door for most of the night. "I'm gonna kill you, red! When they let me out, I'll kill you again!" Most of her rambling didn't make sense, but she definitely scared me. I remember thinking, *This could be me if I don't stop using,* and that thought was probably the most terrifying one I had. I was getting a firsthand look at what life could become if I continued smoking crack, and it was utterly horrifying.

When I got out of jail, I felt helpless. I had ruined the best thing God had ever blessed me with. I had to turn off the self-pity mode and switch to "get shit done" mode.

Allison kept her distance for months until she noticed a real change in me. I had stopped taking Adderall and was consistently taking my prescribed psych meds. For months, we met for lunches and dinners, simply dating again. This was hard for me because I wanted so badly to show her right away that I had changed, but she needed time to really believe it. Time passed, and we grew stronger than ever. Allison was my reason for changing, but I am my reason for continuing to grow. She inspires me daily to be the best version of myself, not just for her but for myself and everyone around me. I've never had someone I care about demand a certain standard from me, and I'm so grateful she saw the light in me before I could see it for myself.

Until her, every relationship I had since childhood revolved around substances in some way. This was the first relationship where drugs were the focus for me, but not for my significant other. As my mood and mental health improved, I was headed in a more positive direction. Even though Allison kept her distance, I wanted to prove to both of us that I could be the person I was capable of being— the person she knew I was capable of being. I could be a better version of myself than I had ever been.

For the first time in my life, I was 100 percent sober. No crutches. No Adderall, no Xanax, no narcotics. Just me— Chelsea—for the first time since I had control over my own life. As I connected with other women in sobriety, joined groups, and attended therapy, I began to see that the world had so much more to offer than just drugs and alcohol. In the past, my experiences were catered to my habits, and I never truly got to experience much because I was shackled by my addiction. I developed new interests and outlets like working out and MMA fighting to help manage my natural aggression. My music started telling a story rather than glorifying the trap lifestyle. I began exploring the world, traveling, and reconnecting with nature. As I grew and changed, Allison became more willing to be involved in my life, and soon, we were inseparable again—but now, for all the right reasons.

Allison and I got married in December 2023 and are now expanding our family. We're going through IVF together, and we should have our first child by September 2025. I'm coming up on 18 months sober, and I have never felt happier or more fulfilled than I do with her every day.

If nothing else, this last relapse taught me that I truly am an addict and alcoholic. Life has changed drastically. When we go out, I don't need to be messed up. Trips are now planned around activities rather than "day-drinking" into the night. I've found a true appreciation for life and the people in it. I have hobbies and goals that I never knew existed, and life is better than I could have ever imagined.

I still have ups and downs, and I still get triggered from time to time. But I'll never forget that losing myself and the life I've built is just one bad choice away. There is no cure for addiction, but you can adopt and develop coping skills that help manage this disease. Using drugs is a negative way of coping that destroys our self-image, self-esteem, and strips us of all self-respect. The underlying issue is often codependency, running amok in our daily lives. Many people who were in active addiction or couldn't provide me with the support I needed are no longer in my life. My circle is much smaller now, but it's filled with people who genuinely care about me and my well-being.

I choose to surround myself only with positive energy and people who support my journey. Above all, I put my sobriety first, which has meant leaving a lot of negative people, places, and things in the past. Making these sacrifices for myself is an absolute necessity because addiction can be sneaky, and you can be triggered at any moment. I try my best to stay away from the people and things that I know will trigger me. Your mental health must come first, above all else—you can't be there for anyone else if you don't have a steady foundation in place for yourself.

Conclusion

Thank you all for taking the time to read my memoir. I hope my struggles and triumphs show you that recovery is possible. It's a 24/7 job with no days off. Breaking the trauma bonds created by our codependency is the only way we can live a life worth living.

For years, I've been confronting my codependency. Just when I think I'm ahead of it, it creeps back in like an unwelcome relative you just can't get rid of. We all have baggage from our past that holds us back from living our best life in the present. We must persevere through the pain to realize that there is glory on the other side.

The word *perseverance* is the most beautiful word in the English language. The definition is as follows:

Perseverance: *Continued effort to do or achieve something despite difficulties, failure, or opposition: the action or condition of persevering: steadfastness.*

Nowhere in this definition does it say that you have to persevere gracefully. Thinking you can save your face and save your ass at the same time is just your pride and ego talking.

As codependents, we've been numbing or denying our feelings for so long that they often come up in overwhelming, overpowering, and agonizing ways. We need to realize that it's necessary to cater to our own personal wants and needs. By doing so, we're being selfish in a healthy way. Because we were taught to suppress our feelings, we need to retrain our brains to understand that speaking up about our wants and needs is actually the healthy thing to do.

Codependents thrive on resentment and self-deprecation. We often overindulge or don't indulge at all, doing things at the extreme ends of every spectrum. As a recovering codependent, the best thing to remember is that there is no black and white. Life exists in the gray area, and most situations don't require a fight-or-flight response. We need to take an extra five seconds before saying or doing anything to avoid misinterpreting situations. Things aren't always personal. Other people's problems are rarely the fault of the codependent, and we need to clean up our own side of the street before approaching anyone else's space with our brooms.

Codependency and addiction are lifelong battles for most. But those who can recognize these issues can live healthy and happy lives with a little extra effort.

No one ever said it would be easy, but God, is it ever worth it.

I'm offering my readers a back-end platform to connect to so they can share their stories, feedback and experiences as well, in hopes that we can all inspire and help each other on our journey to living our best lives. Please visit the Heroin vs. Heroine page on Facebook and become a part of our online community. You can also follow my journey on social media @therealchelzzz on all platforms.

Life is a journey, and we're always learning
Celebrate good times and get lessons from hurting
Always find a message through the messes and cursing
Always move forward cuz there ain't no reversing

Live ya life in wonder
But always ask questions
Cuz life is meant for knowin', and it ain't meant for guessin'
Each and every morning, wakin' up to count my blessin's
And read between the lines until I memorize the lessons

Keep the past behind us, but don't make the same mistakes
Runnin' but they find us wanna keep us in the shade
I can't press rewind on all the choices that I've made
But I'm exorcising demons tryna whip into shape

I'm just goin' wit' the motions
Tryna not to drown inside my ocean of emotions
Fuck makin' a sound. I cause commotion
They should gimme a promotion
But they mad cuz I ain't wit' what they promotin'

Conclusion

Life is a journey, and we're always learning
Celebrate good times and get lessons from hurting
Always find a message through the messes and cursing
Always move forward cuz there ain't no reversing

FOLLOW ME ON ALL SOCIAL MEDIA
AND KEEP UP WITH THE PROGRESS.
THE JOURNEY HAS JUST BEGUN...
@TheRealChelzzz

Thank you for reading my book!

Please Scan the QR code to connect!

I appreciate your interest in my book and value your feedback as it helps me improve future versions of this book. I would appreciate it if you could leave your invaluable review on Amazon.com with your feedback.

Thank you!